FamilyCircle

FABULOUS

Salads

The Family Circle® Promise of Success

Welcome to the world of Confident Cooking,
created for you in the Australian **Family Circle®
Test Kitchen,** where recipes are double-tested by
our team of home economists to achieve a
high standard of success—and delicious
results every time.

MURDOCH BOOKS®

Sydney • London • Vancouver • New York

C O N T E

Italian Pear Salad, page 31

Orange and Fennel Salad, page 54

Tomato Pasta Salad with Thai-style Vegetables, page 110

Caramelised Onion and Potato Salad, page 96

Lime and Prawn Salad, page 88

Gado Gado, page 20

The Publisher thanks the following for their assistance in the photography: Sunbeam Corporation Ltd; Kambrook; Home & Garden on the Mall; Krosno; Maxwell & Williams; Pillivuyt.

Rice Salad, page 9

Beef, Green Bean and Cherry Tomato Salad, page 63

The test kitchen where our recipes are double-tested by our team of home economists to achieve a high standard of success and delicious results every time.

When we test our recipes, we rate them for ease of preparation. The following cookery ratings are on the recipes in this book, making them easy to use and understand.

A single Cooking with Confidence symbol indicates a recipe that is simple and generally quick to make —perfect for beginners.

Two symbols indicate the need for just a little more care and a little more time.

Three symbols indicate special dishes that need more investment in time, care and patience—but the results are worth it.

Front cover: Clockwise, from top: Mixed Seafood Salad, page 77; Tomato and Bocconcini Salad, page 23; Asparagus and Red Capsicum Salad, page 37
Inside front cover: Fennel and Anchovy Salad, page 51

Glossary of Salad Greens

The best salads are made from the freshest seasonal salad leaves and herbs, tossed with a dressing to create a delicious blend of complementary flavours and textures.

SALAD LEAVES

BOK CHOY is a variety of Chinese cabbage with long white stalks and large deep-green leaves. The leaves are crisp with a sweet, cabbage-like flavour. It can be served raw or lightly steamed.

BUTTER LETTUCE has a loosely packed head with soft leaves and a mild flavour. It is also known as butterhead.

CABBAGE is crunchy and slightly sweet when served raw. The most common varieties are plain green cabbage, savoy cabbage with crinkled leaves, red cabbage (shown) and Chinese cabbage.

CHICORY is a long-stemmed plant with dark-green leaves and is often combined with other greens to soften its strong, bitter flavour. It can be eaten raw, or cooked until just wilted for a milder taste.

COS, also know as Romaine, is a large, elongated lettuce with crisp leaves and a slightly sharp flavour.

CURLY ENDIVE is frilly, with narrow prickly leaves. It has a bitter taste, the baby endive having a softer, delicate texture.

ENGLISH SPINACH has dark-green leaves with a long thin stem and a slightly earthy flavour. It should not be confused with silverbeet, which has very large leaves. The young tender leaves are best used in salads. Baby spinach leaves are also available.

FRENCH SPINACH has dark-green leaves with thick stalks. It closely resembles silverbeet, but is much smaller. Young English spinach leaves may be substituted.

MESCLUN is a combination of a variety of baby lettuce leaves and edible flowers. The type of lettuce included will vary according to the season.

MIGNONETTE is from the same family as butter lettuce. It has thinner leaves with red-tinged edges and tends to have a smaller head than butter lettuce.

MIZUNA greens have a mild mustard flavour and are best eaten raw while they are still young. The mature plants have coarser, more serrated leaves.

RADICCHIO is part of the chicory family. It has ruby-red leaves with fine white ribs and the slightly bitter flavour common to the chicory group.

ROCKET, also known as arugula or Italian cress, has a distinct tangy, peppery flavour. The mature leaves have a much stronger flavour and are often too strong to be served on their own.

SPROUTS add flavour and texture to salads and, if fresh and crisp, need no preparation. They are generally sold in punnets, and should be refrigerated and used soon after they are bought as they tend to soften after a few days. Varieties include **alfalfa** (top), **mung bean sprouts** (centre), **snow pea sprouts** (bottom) and **bean sprouts.**

WITLOF, also known as Belgian endive, has smooth, creamy-white leaves with pale yellow or green tips and a slightly bitter taste. There is also a red-tipped variety.

SALAD HERBS

BASIL has a unique strong scent and flavour. It is the main ingredient of pesto and is also used in dressings. Other varieties include sweet basil, purple or opal basil, bush basil and aniseed basil.

CHERVIL is a delicate herb with a slight aniseed taste. It resembles parsley in appearance. Prolonged cooking diminishes its flavour so chervil is best served fresh. There are two varieties, green and red-leafed chervil.

CHIVES are thin, grass-like herbs of the onion family with a hint of onion flavour. The other variety, garlic chives, have a flatter leaf with small white edible flowers and a mild garlic flavour.

CORIANDER, also known as cilantro or Chinese parsley, has a distinctive aroma and fresh, peppery flavour. The whole plant is used—the root, stem and leaves.

DILL is a fern-like herb, similar to fennel, with a delicate, slightly aniseed flavour and aroma. It is delicious in fish salads and vegetable salads.

EDIBLE FLOWERS include geraniums, nasturtiums, rose petals, marigolds, chive flowers, borage flowers and pansies. Choose unsprayed blossoms, preferably from your own garden. They are also available from supermarkets and greengrocers.

FENNEL is a creamy-white, bulbous plant with feathery leaves. The bulbs can be added to salads or cooked as a vegetable and have a sweet, aniseed flavour.

LEMON GRASS is an aromatic herb with a sweet lemon scent. The base and tough outer layers are removed and the white interior is then sliced, chopped or pounded. For salads, use the tender, white portion just above the root.

MARJORAM is a small, green herb, closely related to oregano but with a less peppery flavour.

MINT is a dark-green herb with a strong, fresh flavour. It adds a crisp, fresh taste to salads. Varieties of mint include garden, apple, Vietnamese, pineapple, spearmint and peppermint.

MUSTARD CRESS adds a peppery flavour to salads. Used as a garnish or part of a salad, it is sold in punnets at the seedling stage. Cut off the leaves as needed.

OREGANO is a small-leafed herb with a strong, peppery flavour. It is often used in Greek and Italian dishes.

PARSLEY has a mild celery flavour and is used universally as a garnish. There are two major varieties, curly-leaf (shown) and flat-leaf parsley. Also known as Italian or continental parsley, flat-leaf parsley has a stronger flavour.

SORREL has a large leaf and closely resembles young English spinach. It has a slightly sour taste and lemony aroma. Sorrel should not be prepared using aluminium utensils, as it will discolour.

TARRAGON has a unique, tart flavour and piquant aroma. It is widely used in French cuisine and also to flavour wine vinegars and salad dressings.

THYME is a fragrant herb with tiny pointed leaves and a pungent aroma. The most common varieties are lemon and orange thyme.

WATERCRESS consists of small, round delicate leaves on edible stems with a peppery flavour. Trim away the coarse stems before using.

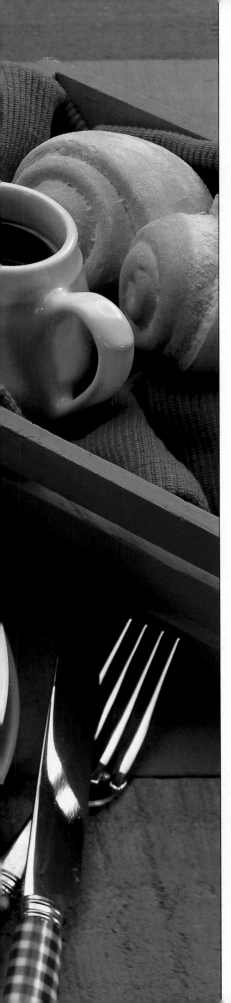

CLASSIC SALADS

CHEF'S SALAD

Preparation time: 25 minutes
Total cooking time: 20 minutes
Serves 4

20 g (³/4 oz) butter
1 tablespoon oil
1 chicken breast fillet
3 eggs
1 iceberg lettuce
2 tomatoes, cut into wedges
2 celery sticks, cut into julienne
    strips (see Note)
150 g (5 oz) ham, cut into thin
    strips
60 g (2 oz) Swiss cheese, cut
    into strips
6 radishes, sliced

Dressing
¹/2 cup (125 ml/4 fl oz) extra
    virgin olive oil
2 tablespoons white wine
    vinegar
1 teaspoon sugar

1 Heat the butter and oil in a small frying pan, add the chicken and cook over medium heat for about 7 minutes on each side, or until the chicken is cooked through. Drain on paper towels, cool and cut into thin strips.

2 Place the eggs in a small pan and cover with cold water. Bring to the boil, stirring occasionally to centre the yolks. Boil for 5 minutes, then drain and plunge into cold water to stop the cooking process. Allow to cool, then peel and cut into wedges.
3 To make the dressing, combine the olive oil, vinegar and sugar in a small jug. Whisk with a small wire whisk or fork until well combined. Season to taste with salt and freshly ground black pepper.
4 Remove and discard the core from the lettuce and coarsely shred the leaves. Divide the shredded lettuce among individual serving plates and top with layers of the tomato, celery, chicken, ham, cheese, egg and radish. Drizzle the dressing over the salad and serve immediately.

NUTRITION PER SERVE
Protein 30 g; Fat 55 g; Carbohydrate 3 g; Dietary Fibre 2 g; Cholesterol 215 mg; 2655 kJ (630 cal)

COOK'S FILE

Note: Julienne strips are even-sized strips of vegetables, the size and shape of matchsticks.
This salad can be prepared without the dressing up to 3 hours in advance. Store, covered, in the refrigerator. Add the dressing just before serving.

Cut the ham and cheese into strips, and cut the celery into julienne strips.

Heat the butter and oil in a frying pan, and add the chicken.

GREEK VILLAGE SALAD

Preparation time: 20 minutes
Total cooking time: Nil
Serves 6–8

6 tomatoes, cut into thin wedges
1 red onion, cut into thin rings
2 Lebanese cucumbers, sliced

1 cup (185 g/6 oz) Kalamata
  olives
200 g (6¹/2 oz) feta cheese
¹/2 cup (125 ml/4 fl oz) extra
  virgin olive oil
dried oregano, to sprinkle

1 Combine the tomato wedges with the onion rings, sliced cucumber and Kalamata olives in a large bowl.

Season to taste with salt and freshly ground black pepper.
2 Break up the feta into large pieces with your fingers and scatter over the top of the salad. Drizzle with the olive oil and sprinkle with some oregano.

NUTRITION PER SERVE (8)
Protein 6 g; Fat 25 g; Carbohydrate 3 g;
Dietary Fibre 2 g; Cholesterol 15 mg;
1060 kJ (250 cal)

Cut the tomatoes into thin wedges, and cut the red onion into thin rings.

Combine the tomato, onion, cucumber and olives in a large bowl.

Using your fingers, break the feta into large pieces.

RICE SALAD

Preparation time: 30 minutes
+ 1 hour refrigeration
Total cooking time: 20 minutes
Serves 6–8

1½ cups (300 g/10 oz) long-
    grain rice
½ cup (80 g/2¾ oz) fresh or
    frozen peas
3 spring onions, sliced
1 green capsicum, finely diced
1 red capsicum, finely diced
310 g (10 oz) can corn kernels
¼ cup (15 g/½ oz) chopped
    mint

Dressing
½ cup (125 ml/4 fl oz) extra
    virgin olive oil
2 tablespoons lemon juice
1 clove garlic, crushed
1 teaspoon sugar

1 Bring a large pan of water to the boil and stir in the rice. Return to the boil and cook for 12–15 minutes, or until tender. Drain and cool.
2 Cook the peas in a small pan of boiling water for about 2 minutes. Rinse under cold water and drain well.
3 To make the dressing, combine the oil, lemon juice, garlic and sugar in a small jug and whisk until well blended. Season with salt and pepper.
4 Combine the rice, peas, spring onion, capsicum, corn and mint in a large bowl. Add the dressing and mix well. Cover and refrigerate for 1 hour. Transfer to a serving dish to serve.

NUTRITION PER SERVE (8)
Protein 5 g; Fat 15 g; Carbohydrate 40 g;
Dietary Fibre 3 g; Cholesterol 0 mg;
1350 kJ (320 cal)

Slice the spring onions and finely dice the capsicums, removing the white membrane.

Cook the peas in a pan of boiling water for 2 minutes.

Combine the rice, vegetables and mint and drizzle with the dressing.

SALAD NICOISE

Preparation time: 30 minutes
Total cooking time: 25 minutes
Serves 4–6

4 eggs
500 g (1 lb) baby new potatoes
250 g (8 oz) green beans,
    topped and tailed
6 artichoke hearts in oil, drained
350 g (11¼ oz) mesclun
    (assorted salad leaves)
4 tomatoes, cut into wedges
425 g (13½ oz) can tuna,
    drained and broken into
    chunks
1 red capsicum, cut into strips
1 tablespoon bottled capers,
    drained
1 tablespoon coarsely chopped
    fresh tarragon
10 Niçoise (small) olives

Dressing
1 clove garlic, crushed
3 teaspoons Dijon mustard
2 anchovy fillets in oil, drained
    and finely chopped
¼ cup (60 ml/2 fl oz) white
    wine vinegar
½ cup (125 ml/4 fl oz) extra
    virgin olive oil

1 Put the eggs in a pan of water and bring to the boil, stirring occasionally to centre the yolks. Boil for 5 minutes, drain and cool in cold water. Peel and cut into wedges.
2 Boil the potatoes until tender, drain and cool. Cut into thick slices. Plunge the beans into a pan of boiling water, return to the boil for 2 minutes, then drain and rinse under cold water. Chill in a bowl of iced water. Halve or quarter the artichokes.
3 Arrange the mesclun on a serving platter or individual plates. Top with the potato, beans, tomato, artichoke, tuna, egg and capsicum. Sprinkle with the capers, tarragon and olives.
4 To make the dressing, use a food processor or whisk to mix the garlic, mustard, anchovies and vinegar until smooth. Gradually add the oil and blend until smooth. Season with salt and pepper, and drizzle over the salad.

NUTRITION PER SERVE (6)
Protein 30 g; Fat 25 g; Carbohydrate 15 g; Dietary Fibre 7 g; Cholesterol 160 mg; 1760 kJ (420 cal)

Top and tail the green beans, and cut the tomatoes into wedges.

Leave the cooked beans in a bowl of iced water until cold.

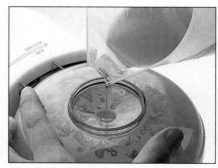

Gradually add the oil to the blended garlic, mustard, anchovies and vinegar.

GREEN SALAD

Preparation time: 20 minutes
Total cooking time: Nil
Serves 8

500 g (1 lb) watercress
150 g (5 oz) rocket
1 butter lettuce
2 small avocados
60 g (2 oz) snow pea sprouts
2 spring onions, sliced
2 Lebanese cucumbers, sliced

Mustard Dressing
1/2 cup (125 ml/4 fl oz) extra
    virgin olive oil
2 tablespoons white wine
    vinegar
1 tablespoon lemon juice
1 tablespoon Dijon or
    wholegrain mustard
1 clove garlic, crushed
1 teaspoon sugar

1 Trim the tough ends from the watercress and rocket. Wash well and place on a tea towel to drain.
2 Remove the central core from the lettuce, wash and drain on a tea towel or use a salad spinner to dry the leaves thoroughly.
3 Cut the avocados into large pieces, reserving some long slices for garnishing. Put the watercress, rocket, snow pea sprouts, lettuce, avocado, spring onion and cucumber in a large bowl and toss very gently.
4 To make the dressing, put the oil, vinegar, lemon juice, mustard, garlic and sugar in a small jug and whisk with a small wire whisk or a fork until the ingredients are well blended. Season to taste with salt and freshly ground black pepper. Arrange the

salad in a large serving bowl or on a large platter. Drizzle the dressing over the salad and serve garnished with the reserved avocado slices.

NUTRITION PER SERVE
Protein 4 g; Fat 30 g; Carbohydrate 3 g; Dietary Fibre 5 g; Cholesterol 0 mg; 1195 kJ (285 cal)

COOK'S FILE

Note: Serve this salad immediately or the avocado will brown.
To test if an avocado is ripe, very gently push the stem. If it gives way easily, the avocado is ready to eat. Purchase underripe avocados and ripen them at room temperature.

Halve the cucumbers lengthways, then cut into diagonal slices.

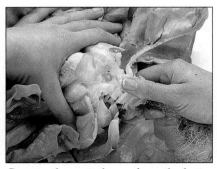

Remove the central core from the butter lettuce, then wash and drain well.

Whisk the dressing ingredients in a small jug and season with salt and pepper.

HOT POTATO SALAD

Preparation time: 15 minutes
Total cooking time: 30 minutes
Serves 6–8

4 rashers bacon (optional)
1¹/2 kg (3 lb) small Desiree
  potatoes (or other small,
  waxy, red-skinned potatoes)
4 spring onions, sliced
¹/4 cup (7 g/¹/4 oz) chopped flat-
  leaf parsley
¹/2 teaspoon salt

Dressing
²/3 cup (170 ml/5¹/2 fl oz) extra
  virgin olive oil
1 tablespoon Dijon mustard
¹/3 cup (80 ml/2³/4 fl oz) white
  wine vinegar

1 Trim the rind and excess fat from the bacon. Cook under a hot grill until crisp. Chop into small pieces.
2 Bring a large heavy-based pan of water to the boil. Add the potatoes and simmer until just tender, trying not to let the skins break away too much. Drain and cool slightly.
3 To make the dressing, whisk the ingredients in a jug until well blended.
4 Cut the potatoes into quarters and place in a large bowl with half the bacon, the spring onion, parsley, salt and some freshly ground black pepper. Pour in half the dressing and toss gently to coat the potatoes.
5 Transfer to a serving bowl, drizzle with the remaining dressing and sprinkle with the remaining bacon.

NUTRITION PER SERVE (8)
Protein 8 g; Fat 20 g; Carbohydrate 25 g;
Dietary Fibre 3 g; Cholesterol 10 mg;
1365 kJ (325 cal)

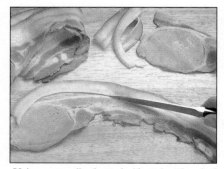

Using a small, sharp knife, trim the rind and excess fat from the bacon.

Whisk the dressing ingredients in a small jug until well blended.

When the potatoes are just cool enough to handle, cut them into quarters.

SPINACH SALAD

Preparation time: 20 minutes
Total cooking time: 20 minutes
Serves 2–4

3 slices white bread, crusts
   removed
150 g (5 oz) English spinach
   leaves
2–3 tablespoons pine nuts
3 rashers bacon, chopped
8 button mushrooms, finely
   sliced
1/4 cup (7 g/1/4 oz) basil leaves,
   shredded

1–2 cloves garlic, crushed
2–3 tablespoons olive oil
balsamic vinegar or freshly
   squeezed lemon juice,
   to taste

1 Preheat the oven to moderately hot 190°C (375°F/Gas 5). Cut the bread into small cubes, spread on a baking tray and bake for 10 minutes, or until the bread cubes are golden.
2 Gently rinse the spinach leaves under cold water. Bundle them in a clean tea towel and shake gently to remove the water. Tear into pieces and place in a large serving bowl. Put the pine nuts in a non-stick frying pan

and stir gently over low heat until golden brown. Remove and cool slightly. Add the bacon to the pan and cook for 5–6 minutes, or until crispy. Remove and drain on paper towels.
3 Add the pine nuts, bacon, bread cubes, mushrooms and basil to the spinach leaves. Whisk the garlic and oil together and pour over the salad, mixing gently. Drizzle with the vinegar or lemon juice. Sprinkle with salt and freshly ground pepper, and serve immediately.

NUTRITION PER SERVE (4)
Protein 10 g; Fat 20 g; Carbohydrate 10 g; Dietary Fibre 3 g; Cholesterol 15 mg; 1105 kJ (265 cal)

Cut the bread into small cubes and spread on a baking tray.

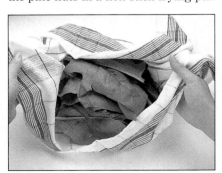

Bundle the spinach leaves in a tea towel and shake to remove the excess water.

Pour the combined garlic and oil over the salad, mixing gently.

13

THAI BEEF SALAD WITH MINT AND CORIANDER

Preparation time: 40 minutes
Total cooking time: 4 minutes
Serves 6

2 tablespoons dried shrimp
125 g (4 oz) English spinach
1 tablespoon sesame oil
500 g (1 lb) rump steak
1 cup (90 g/3 oz) bean sprouts
1 small red onion, thinly sliced
1 small red capsicum, cut into
    thin strips
1 small Lebanese cucumber, cut
    into thin strips
200 g (6¹/₂ oz) daikon radish,
    peeled and cut into thin
    strips
1 small tomato, halved, seeded
    and thinly sliced
¹/₄ cup (5 g/¹/₄ oz) mint leaves
¹/₂ cup (15 g/¹/₂ oz) coriander
    leaves
2 cloves garlic, finely chopped
1–2 small red chillies, chopped
2 small green chillies, chopped

Dressing
¹/₄ cup (60 ml/2 fl oz) lime juice
¹/₄ cup (60 ml/2 fl oz) fish sauce
1 tablespoon finely chopped
    lemon grass
1 teaspoon sugar

1 Soak the dried shrimp in hot water for 15 minutes; drain well and chop finely. Wash the English spinach and drain well. Trim the thick stalks and coarsely shred the leaves.
2 Heat the oil in a frying pan, add the steak and cook over high heat until medium rare, for about 1¹/₂–2 minutes on each side. Remove from the pan and allow to cool slightly. Slice the steak thinly.
3 To make the dressing, combine the lime juice, fish sauce, lemon grass and sugar in a small jug. Whisk until the ingredients are well combined.
4 To assemble the salad, combine the shrimp, sliced beef, bean sprouts, onion, capsicum, cucumber, radish, tomato, mint, coriander, garlic and chillies in a large bowl. Place the spinach on a serving plate, top with the combined beef and vegetables, and drizzle with the dressing.

NUTRITION PER SERVE
Protein 25 g; Fat 6 g; Carbohydrate 6 g; Dietary Fibre 4 g; Cholesterol 65 mg; 730 kJ (175 cal)

Slice the onion, and cut the capsicum, cucumber and daikon into thin strips.

Trim the thick stalks from the English spinach and coarsely shred the leaves.

Cook the steak over high heat until it is medium rare.

BEAN SALAD

Preparation time: 30 minutes
Total cooking time: 5 minutes
Serves 8–10

250 g (8 oz) green beans,
    topped and tailed
400 g (12³/4 oz) can chickpeas,
    drained and rinsed
425 g (13¹/2 oz) can red kidney
    beans, drained and rinsed
400 g (12³/4 oz) can cannellini
    beans, drained and rinsed
270 g (8³/4 oz) can corn kernels,
    drained and rinsed
3 spring onions, sliced
1 red capsicum, finely chopped
3 celery sticks, chopped
4–6 gherkins, chopped
    (optional)
¹/4 cup (15 g/¹/2 oz) chopped
    mint
¹/4 cup (7 g/¹/4 oz) chopped flat-
    leaf parsley

Mustard Vinaigrette
1 quantity Basic Vinaigrette
    (see page 18)
1 tablespoon Dijon mustard
1 clove garlic, crushed

1 Cut the green beans into short
lengths. Bring a small pan of water to
the boil, add the beans and cook for
2 minutes. Drain and rinse under cold
water then leave in a bowl of iced
water until cold. Drain well.
2 Place the beans, chickpeas, kidney
beans, cannellini beans, corn, spring
onion, capsicum, celery, gherkin, mint
and parsley in a large bowl. Season
with salt and freshly ground black
pepper and mix until well combined.
3 To make the Mustard Vinaigrette,
whisk together the Basic Vinaigrette,
mustard and crushed garlic until
combined. Drizzle over the salad and
toss gently to combine. Transfer to a
large serving bowl or platter.

NUTRITION PER SERVE (10)
Protein 10 g; Fat 15 g; Carbohydrate 25 g;
Dietary Fibre 10 g; Cholesterol 0 mg;
1090 kJ (260 cal)

COOK'S FILE

Note: Prepare the salad up to 3 hours
in advance, cover and refrigerate. Add
the dressing just before serving.

*Cut the vegetables into small dice, trying
to make them all a similar size.*

*Add the beans to a pan of boiling water
and cook for 2 minutes.*

CAESAR SALAD

Preparation time: 15 minutes
Total cooking time: 20 minutes
Serves 4

4 slices white bread, crusts
   removed, cubed
3 rashers bacon, chopped
1 cos lettuce
50 g (1¾ oz) Parmesan
   shavings
Parmesan shavings, extra

Dressing
2–4 anchovies
1 egg
2 tablespoons lemon juice
1 clove garlic, crushed
½ cup (125 ml/4 fl oz) olive oil

1 Preheat the oven to moderately hot 190°C (375°F/Gas 5). Spread the bread cubes on a baking tray and bake for 15 minutes, or until golden.
2 Cook the bacon over medium heat until it is crisp. Drain on paper towels.
3 Tear the lettuce leaves into pieces and put in a serving bowl with the bread cubes, bacon and Parmesan.
4 To make the dressing, process the anchovies, egg, lemon juice and garlic in a food processor for 20 seconds, or until smooth. With the motor running, add the oil in a thin stream until the dressing is thick and creamy. Drizzle over the salad, sprinkle with the extra Parmesan and serve immediately.

NUTRITION PER SERVE
Protein 20 g; Fat 40 g; Carbohydrate 15 g;
Dietary Fibre 2 g; Cholesterol 80 mg;
2015 kJ (480 cal)

Stir the bacon over medium heat until it is crisp.

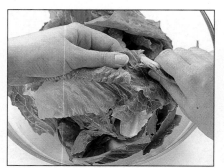

Using your fingers, tear the lettuce leaves into pieces.

Blend the anchovies, egg, lemon juice and garlic in a food processor.

Top row: Basic Vinaigrette; Basil Garlic Dressing; Ginger and Sesame Dressing; Balsamic Dressing
Bottom row: Lemon Soy Dressing; Blue Cheese Dressing; Chilli Lime Dressing; Thousand Island Dressing

GINGER AND SESAME DRESSING

Put 1 teaspoon sesame oil, 3 teaspoons rice wine vinegar, 1 teaspoon finely grated orange rind, 2 tablespoons orange juice and 2 teaspoons grated fresh ginger in a small jug. Gradually whisk in $1/2$ cup (125 ml/4 fl oz) vegetable oil until well blended. Season with salt and freshly ground black pepper. Makes about $3/4$ cup (185 ml/6 fl oz)

NUTRITION PER 100 g: Protein 0 g; Fat 65 g; Carbohydrate 2 g; Dietary Fibre 0 g; Cholesterol 0 mg; 2460 kJ (585 cal)

CHILLI LIME DRESSING

Put $1/4$ cup (60 ml/2 fl oz) lime juice, 2 tablespoons fish sauce, 1–2 teaspoons sambal oelek and 1 teaspoon sugar in a small jug. Using a small wire whisk or fork, gradually whisk in $1/4$ cup (60 ml/2 fl oz) vegetable oil in a thin stream until well blended. Makes about $3/4$ cup (185 ml/6 fl oz)

NUTRITION PER 100 g: Protein 2 g; Fat 35 g; Carbohydrate 4 g; Dietary Fibre 0 g; Cholesterol 0 mg; 1365 kJ (325 cal)

BALSAMIC DRESSING

Whisk 2 tablespoons balsamic vinegar and 1 teaspoon French mustard in a small jug until combined. Gradually beat in $1/3$ cup (80 ml/$2^3/4$ fl oz) extra virgin olive oil. Season with salt and freshly ground black pepper. Cut 1 small clove garlic in half, skewer onto a toothpick and leave in the dressing to infuse for at least 1 hour. Makes about $1/2$ cup (125 ml/4 fl oz)

NUTRITION PER 100 g: Protein 0 g; Fat 55 g; Carbohydrate 0 g; Dietary Fibre 1 g; Cholesterol 0 mg; 2145 kJ (510 cal)

THOUSAND ISLAND DRESSING

Put $1/2$ cup whole egg mayonnaise, 1 tablespoon tomato paste, 1 teaspoon Worcestershire sauce, 1 teaspoon French mustard and 2 teaspoons chilli sauce in a small bowl and stir until well combined. Season with salt. Makes about $1/2$ cup (125 ml/4 fl oz)

NUTRITION PER 100 g: Protein 1 g; Fat 25 g; Carbohydrate 20 g; Dietary Fibre 1 g; Cholesterol 25 mg; 1265 kJ (300 cal)

19

GADO GADO

Preparation time: 30 minutes
Total cooking time: 35 minutes
Serves 4

6 new potatoes
2 carrots, cut into thick strips
250 g (8 oz) snake beans, cut
    into 10 cm (4 inch) lengths
2 tablespoons peanut oil
250 g (8 oz) firm tofu, cubed
100 g (3¼ oz) baby English
    spinach leaves
2 Lebanese cucumbers, cut into
    thick strips
1 large red capsicum, cut into
    thick strips
100 g (3¼ oz) bean sprouts
5 hard-boiled eggs

Peanut Sauce
1 tablespoon peanut oil
1 onion, finely chopped
²/₃ cup (160 g/5¼ oz) peanut
    butter
¼ cup (60 ml/2 fl oz) kecap
    manis
2 tablespoons ground coriander
2 teaspoons chilli sauce
¾ cup (185 ml/6 fl oz) coconut
    cream
1 teaspoon grated palm sugar
1 tablespoon lemon juice

1 Cook the potatoes in boiling water until tender. Drain and cool slightly. Cut into quarters. Cook the carrots and beans separately in pans of boiling water until just tender. Plunge into iced water, then drain.
2 Heat the oil in a non-stick frying pan and cook the tofu in batches until crisp. Drain on paper towels.
3 To make the peanut sauce, heat the oil in a pan over low heat and cook the onion for 5 minutes, or until golden. Add the peanut butter, kecap manis, coriander, chilli sauce and coconut cream. Bring to the boil, reduce the heat and simmer for 5 minutes. Stir in the sugar and juice until dissolved.
4 Arrange the vegetables and tofu on a plate. Halve the eggs and place in the centre. Serve with the sauce.

NUTRITION PER SERVE
Protein 35 g; Fat 55 g; Carbohydrate 35 g; Dietary Fibre 15 g; Cholesterol 265 mg; 3175 kJ (755 cal)

Cut the cucumbers and capsicum into thick strips.

Cook the snake beans quickly in a pan of boiling water.

Heat the oil and cook the tofu in batches until crisp and golden brown.

Add the peanut butter, kecap manis, coriander, chilli sauce and coconut cream.

COLESLAW

Preparation time: 20 minutes
Total cooking time: Nil
Serves 8–10

1/2 **green (savoy) cabbage**
1/4 **red cabbage**
3 **carrots, coarsely grated**
6 **radishes, coarsely grated**
1 **red capsicum, chopped**
4 **spring onions, sliced**

1/4 **cup (15 g/1/2 oz) chopped flat-leaf parsley**
1 **cup (250 g/8 oz) mayonnaise**

1 Remove the hard cores from the cabbages and shred the leaves with a sharp knife. Place in a large bowl.
2 Add the carrot, radish, capsicum, spring onion and parsley to the bowl with the cabbage.
3 Add the mayonnaise, season with salt and freshly ground black pepper and toss until well combined.

NUTRITION PER SERVE (10)
Protein 5 g; Fat 10 g; Carbohydrate 10 g; Dietary Fibre 10 g; Cholesterol 8 mg; 610 kJ (145 cal)

COOK'S FILE

Variation: As an alternative to mayonnaise, the coleslaw could be dressed with one quantity of the Chilli Lime Dressing, see page 19.
Cover and refrigerate the chopped vegetables for up to 3 hours before serving. Add the mayonnaise just before serving the coleslaw.

Coarsely grate the carrots and the radishes using a metal grater.

Remove the hard cores from the cabbages with a sharp knife.

Add the mayonnaise and season with salt and freshly ground black pepper.

POTATO SALAD

Preparation time: 30 minutes
Total cooking time: 5 minutes
Serves 4

600 g (1 1/4 lb) potatoes, cut into
    bite-sized pieces
1 small onion, finely chopped
1 small green capsicum, chopped
2–3 celery sticks, finely
    chopped
1/4 cup (15 g/1/2 oz) finely
    chopped parsley

Dressing
3/4 cup (185 g/6 oz) mayonnaise
1–2 tablespoons vinegar or
    lemon juice
2 tablespoons sour cream

1 Cook the potato in a large pan of boiling water for 5 minutes, or until just tender (pierce with a small sharp knife—if the potato comes away easily it is ready). Drain and cool completely.

2 Combine the onion, capsicum, celery and parsley, reserving some for garnishing, with the cooled potato in a large salad bowl.

3 To make the dressing, mix together the mayonnaise, vinegar and sour cream. Season with salt and pepper. Pour over the salad and toss gently to combine, without breaking the potato. Garnish with the remaining parsley.

NUTRITION PER SERVE
Protein 6 g; Fat 20 g; Carbohydrate 30 g;
Dietary Fibre 4 g; Cholesterol 30 mg;
1355 kJ (320 cal)

COOK'S FILE

Note: Any potato is suitable for this recipe. Most potatoes are delicious with their skins left on.

Cut the potatoes into bite-sized pieces, leaving the skins on.

Combine the onion, capsicum, celery and parsley with the cooled potato.

Mix together the mayonnaise, vinegar and sour cream and season, to taste.

TOMATO AND BOCCONCINI SALAD

Preparation time: 15 minutes
Total cooking time: Nil
Serves 4

6 egg (Roma) tomatoes
5 bocconcini
2/3 cup (20 g/3/4 oz) loosely
    packed basil leaves

Dressing
1/4 cup (60 ml/2 fl oz) extra
    virgin olive oil
2 tablespoons balsamic vinegar

1 Cut the tomatoes lengthways into 3–4 slices (discard the thin outside slices, which won't lie flat). Slice the bocconcini lengthways into 3–4 slices.
2 Arrange some tomato slices on a serving plate, place a bocconcini slice on top of each tomato and scatter with some of the basil leaves. Repeat the layers until all the tomato, bocconcini and basil have been used. Season with salt and pepper.
3 To make the dressing, whisk the oil and vinegar. Drizzle over the salad.

NUTRITION PER SERVE
Protein 10 g; Fat 25 g; Carbohydrate 3 g; Dietary Fibre 2 g; Cholesterol 25 mg; 1080 kJ (255 cal)

COOK'S FILE

Variation: Try the salad with a pesto dressing. Process 1/2 cup (25 g/3/4 oz) basil leaves, 1 tablespoon pine nuts, 1/4 cup (25 g/3/4 oz) grated Parmesan and 1 crushed clove garlic in a food processor until finely chopped. With the motor running, add 1/4 cup (60 ml/ 2 fl oz) olive oil and 1 tablespoon lemon juice in a steady stream.

Slice the tomatoes lengthways, discarding the thin outside slices.

Slice the bocconcini lengthways into 3–4 slices.

Whisk together the olive oil and balsamic vinegar in a small jug.

23

TABOULI

Preparation time: 40 minutes
Total cooking time: Nil
Serves 4

3/4 cup (130 g/4¼ oz) burghul
2 large tomatoes, chopped
4 spring onions, finely chopped
1 yellow capsicum, finely
    chopped
1½ cups (45 g/1½ oz) chopped
    flat-leaf parsley
¼ cup (15 g/½ oz) chopped
    mint

Dressing
¼ cup (60 ml/2 fl oz) olive oil
¼ cup (60 ml/2 fl oz) lemon
    juice
1 clove garlic, crushed

1 Place the burghul in a medium bowl and cover with ¾ cup (185 ml/ 6 fl oz) of boiling water. Leave for 30 minutes, or until all the water is absorbed and the grains have swollen.
2 In a clean bowl combine the tomato, spring onion, capsicum, herbs and burghul. Season to taste with salt and freshly ground black pepper.
3 To make the dressing, whisk the oil, lemon juice and garlic in a jug until well blended. Pour over the salad and toss well.

NUTRITION PER SERVE
Protein 5 g; Fat 15 g; Carbohydrate 25 g; Dietary Fibre 7 g; Cholesterol 0 mg; 1045 kJ (250 cal)

COOK'S FILE

Note: Burghul is cracked wheat, and is also known as bulgar wheat.
This traditional Lebanese salad is especially good as a sandwich filling.

Finely chop the yellow capsicum, removing the seeds and white membrane.

Place the burghul in a bowl and cover with the boiling water.

Combine the tomato, spring onion, capsicum, herbs and burghul.

WALDORF SALAD

Preparation time: 20 minutes
Total cooking time: Nil
Serves 4–6

2 green apples
2 red apples
2 tablespoons lemon juice
¼ cup (30 g/1 oz) walnut pieces
4 celery sticks, sliced

1 cup (250 g/8 oz) mayonnaise
lettuce, to serve (optional)

1 Quarter the apples, remove and discard the seeds and cores, and cut the apples into small pieces.
2 Place the apple in a large bowl, drizzle with the lemon juice and toss to coat and prevent the apples discolouring. Add the walnut pieces and celery and mix well.
3 Add the mayonnaise to the apple

mixture and toss until well coated. Spoon the salad into a lettuce-lined bowl and serve immediately.

NUTRITION PER SERVE (6)
Protein 2 g; Fat 15 g; Carbohydrate 20 g; Dietary Fibre 3 g; Cholesterol 15 mg; 1020 kJ (240 cal)

COOK'S FILE

Note: This salad may be made up to 2 hours in advance and stored, covered, in the refrigerator.

Quarter the apples, remove the seeds and cut into small pieces.

Pour the lemon juice over the apples and toss to coat.

Add the mayonnaise to the apple mixture and toss until well coated.

MIXED LEAF SALAD

Preparation time: 20 minutes
Total cooking time: Nil
Serves 6–8

Dressing
1 clove garlic, halved
1/2 cup (125 ml/4 fl oz) extra
    virgin olive oil
2 tablespoons white wine
    vinegar
2 teaspoons Dijon mustard
1/2 teaspoon sugar

50 g (1³/4 oz) snow pea sprouts
150 g (5 oz) mixed lettuce
    leaves
80 g (2³/4 oz) baby English
    spinach leaves
50 g (1³/4 oz) edible flower
    petals

1 To make the dressing, skewer the garlic onto a toothpick and sit it in a jug with the combined oil, vinegar, mustard and sugar. Leave the garlic to infuse while preparing the salad.
2 Trim the ends from the snow pea sprouts. Rinse the lettuce and spinach

leaves under running water and drain well. Toss with the snow pea sprouts and flowers in a large bowl, cover with plastic wrap and refrigerate until ready to serve.
3 To serve, remove and discard the garlic clove from the dressing, whisk until well blended and season with salt and freshly ground black pepper. Place the salad in a serving bowl and drizzle with the dressing.

NUTRITION PER SERVE (8)
Protein 1 g; Fat 15 g; Carbohydrate 1 g;
Dietary Fibre 1 g; Cholesterol 0 mg;
585 kJ (140 cal)

Carefully separate the petals from the edible flowers.

Skewer the garlic onto a toothpick and allow it to infuse into the dressing.

Drizzle the dressing over the tossed salad in a serving bowl.

PRAWN SALAD

Preparation time: 20 minutes
+ 1 hour chilling
Total cooking time: Nil
Serves 4

2 tablespoons olive oil
2 tablespoons lemon juice
24 cooked king prawns
1 Lebanese cucumber
2 tablespoons coarsely chopped
   flat-leaf parsley
cos lettuce leaves, to serve
1 quantity Thousand Island
   Dressing (see page 19)

1 Place the olive oil and lemon juice in a screw-top jar, season with salt and freshly ground black pepper and shake until well blended.
2 Peel and devein the prawns, keeping the tails intact. Halve the cucumber lengthways and slice very thinly.
3 Combine the olive oil mixture, prawns, cucumber and parsley in a bowl. Cover and refrigerate for 1 hour.
4 To serve, arrange the salad on individual plates lined with cos lettuce leaves, and serve with the Thousand Island Dressing.

NUTRITION PER SERVE
Protein 25 g; Fat 20 g; Carbohydrate 7 g; Dietary Fibre 1 g; Cholesterol 190 mg; 1210 kJ (290 cal)

COOK'S FILE

Variation: Try this salad with a hint of Asian flavours. Substitute lime juice for the lemon juice, use coriander instead of the parsley and add 1 finely chopped red chilli, 2 teaspoons fish sauce and 2 teaspoons grated fresh ginger. Omit the Thousand Island Dressing and serve with avocado slices.

Place the oil and lemon juice in a screw-top jar and season with salt and pepper.

Halve the cucumbers lengthways, and cut into very thin slices.

Make up 1 quantity of the Thousand Island Dressing, to serve.

GARDEN GREENS

WARM ASPARAGUS AND EGG SALAD

Preparation time: 15 minutes
Total cooking time: 15 minutes
Serves 4

Dressing
¹/₄ cup (60 ml/2 fl oz) extra
    virgin olive oil
1 tablespoon lemon juice
1 clove garlic, crushed

4 eggs, at room temperature
    (see Note)
310 g (10 oz) fresh asparagus
8 anchovy fillets
1 teaspoon cracked black
    pepper
Parmesan shavings, to serve

1 To make the dressing, put the olive oil, lemon juice and garlic in a small jug and whisk with a small wire whisk or a fork to combine. Season with salt, to taste.
2 Half fill a saucepan with water and heat until simmering. Add the eggs and cook for 6–7 minutes, stirring occasionally to centre the yolks. The yolks should be set, but not too firm. Drain and cover with cold water for a few minutes, then peel off the shells while the eggs are still warm.
3 Trim the woody ends from the asparagus by bending the stem of each spear. Plunge the asparagus into a large frying pan of boiling water and cook for 3 minutes, or until just tender. Drain and pat dry with paper towels. Divide among individual serving plates.
4 Cut the eggs in half. Drain the anchovy fillets on paper towels and arrange with the eggs over the warm asparagus. Sprinkle with the cracked black pepper. Re-whisk the dressing and drizzle over the salad. Serve with shavings of Parmesan.

NUTRITION PER SERVE
Protein 15 g; Fat 25 g; Carbohydrate 1 g; Dietary Fibre 1 g; Cholesterol 195 mg; 1115 kJ (265 cal)

COOK'S FILE

Note: If the eggs have been brought to room temperature before they are added to the simmering water, they are less likely to crack during cooking.
Hint: To make Parmesan shavings, have a block of Parmesan at room temperature. This will prevent it from cracking as you make the curls. Draw a vegetable peeler across the block to make shavings.

To remove the woody ends from the asparagus, bend the stem of each spear.

Plunge the asparagus into a frying pan of boiling water.

LEMON, FENNEL AND ROCKET SALAD

Preparation time: 25 minutes
Total cooking time: 5 minutes
Serves 4

2 lemons
2 oranges
1 large fennel bulb or 2 baby
   fennel
200 g (6½ oz) rocket
100 g (3¼ oz) pecans, chopped
½ cup (85 g/2¾ oz) stuffed
   green olives, halved
   lengthwise

Toasted Sesame Dressing
1 tablespoon sesame oil
1 tablespoon sesame seeds
¼ cup (60 ml/2 fl oz) olive oil
2 tablespoons white wine
   vinegar
1 teaspoon French mustard

1 Peel the lemons and oranges, removing all the white pith. Cut into thin slices and remove any seeds. Thinly slice the fennel. Wash and dry the rocket and tear into pieces. Chill while making the dressing.
2 To make the dressing, heat the oil in a small pan over moderate heat. Add the sesame seeds and fry, stirring constantly, until lightly golden. Remove from the heat and cool. Pour the mixture into a small jug, whisk in the remaining ingredients and season with salt and ground black pepper.
3 Combine the fruit, fennel, rocket, pecans and olives in a shallow serving bowl. Drizzle with the dressing.

NUTRITION PER SERVE
Protein 6 g; Fat 40 g; Carbohydrate 10 g; Dietary Fibre 9 g; Cholesterol 0 mg; 1820 kJ (435 cal)

COOK'S FILE

Note: Blood oranges have a lovely tart flavour and, when in season, are delicious in this recipe.

Cut the peeled lemons and oranges into thin slices and remove any seeds.

Using a large, sharp knife, thinly slice the fennel crossways.

Stir the sesame seeds in the sesame oil until they are lightly golden.

ITALIAN PEAR SALAD

Preparation time: 20 minutes
Total cooking time: Nil
Serves 4

4 ripe green or red pears
250 g (8 oz) bocconcini, sliced
4 thin slices prosciutto, cut into
    bite-sized pieces
4 fresh figs, quartered
1/4 cup (30 g/1 oz) walnut
    pieces

Dressing
1/4 cup (60 ml/2 fl oz) extra
    virgin olive oil
1/4 teaspoon finely grated lemon
    rind
1 tablespoon lemon juice
1 tablespoon chopped chives

1 Cut the pears into quarters and use a melon baller or teaspoon to remove the cores. Arrange the pears in a serving dish and scatter with the sliced bocconcini, prosciutto, figs and walnut pieces.

2 To make the dressing, put the oil, lemon rind and juice, and chives in a small bowl and whisk to combine. Season with salt and pepper, to taste. Drizzle the dressing over the salad and serve immediately.

NUTRITION PER SERVE
Protein 30 g; Fat 40 g; Carbohydrate 25 g; Dietary Fibre 6 g; Cholesterol 70 mg; 2495 kJ (595 cal)

COOK'S FILE

Note: If fresh figs are unavailable or out of season, use dried figs.

Using a large sharp knife, cut each bocconcini into about 4 slices.

Using a sharp knife, cut the fresh figs into quarters.

Cut the pears into quarters and use a melon baller to remove the cores.

STUFFED MUSHROOM SALAD

Preparation time: 25 minutes
Total cooking time: Nil
Serves 4

20 button mushrooms
1/4 cup (60 g/2 oz) pesto, chilled
100 g (3 1/4 oz) rocket leaves
1 green oakleaf lettuce
12 small black olives
1/3 cup (50 g/1 3/4 oz) sliced
    semi-dried or sun-dried
    tomatoes
1 tablespoon coarsely chopped
    basil
Parmesan shavings, to serve

Dressing
1/3 cup (80 ml/2 3/4 fl oz) olive oil
1 tablespoon white wine vinegar
1 teaspoon Dijon mustard

1 Trim the mushroom stalks level with the caps and scoop out the remaining stalk using a melon baller. Spoon the pesto into the mushrooms.
2 To make the dressing, place the ingredients in a small bowl and whisk to combine. Season with salt and pepper, to taste.
3 Arrange the rocket and lettuce leaves on a serving plate and top with the mushrooms, olives, tomato and basil. Drizzle the dressing over the salad and top with the Parmesan shavings. Serve immediately.

NUTRITION PER SERVE
Protein 9 g; Fat 35 g; Carbohydrate 2 g;
Dietary Fibre 3 g; Cholesterol 15 mg;
1525 kJ (365 cal)

COOK'S FILE

Hint: Homemade pesto is preferable for this recipe. To make your own, process 1 cup (30 g/1 oz) loosely packed basil leaves, 2 tablespoons pine nuts and 1/4 cup (25 g/3/4 oz) grated Parmesan in a food processor to form a smooth paste. Gradually pour in 1/4 cup (60 ml/2 fl oz) olive oil in a steady stream with the motor running. Process until combined.
Note: Semi sun-dried tomatoes are brighter and more succulent than sun-dried tomatoes, giving your salad more colour.

Draw a vegetable peeler across a block of Parmesan to make the shavings.

Trim the mushroom stalks so they are level with the caps.

Spoon the chilled pesto into the mushroom caps.

JAPANESE SPINACH SALAD

Preparation time: 25 minutes
Total cooking time: 5 minutes
Serves 4

2 eggs
1 sheet nori, cut into
    matchsticks
100 g (3¼ oz) baby English
    spinach leaves
1 small red onion, finely sliced
½ small daikon radish, finely
    sliced
2 Lebanese cucumbers, sliced
30 g (1 oz) pickled ginger, sliced
1 tablespoon toasted sesame
    seeds

Dressing
⅓ cup (80 ml/2¾ fl oz) light
    olive oil
1 tablespoon rice vinegar
1 tablespoon light soy sauce

1 Preheat the grill to hot. Beat the eggs lightly in a small bowl, add 1 tablespoon water and the nori. Season with salt and pepper. Heat and grease a 20 cm (8 inch) omelette pan. Pour in the egg mixture to make a thin omelette. When lightly browned underneath, place under the grill to set the top, without colouring. Turn out onto a board and leave to cool. Cut the omelette into thin strips.
2 To make the dressing, put the olive oil, vinegar and soy sauce in a small bowl. Whisk gently to combine with a small wire whisk or a fork.
3 Put the spinach leaves, onion, daikon, cucumber, pickled ginger, toasted sesame seeds and omelette strips in a large serving bowl. Add the dressing and toss the salad gently to combine. Serve immediately.

NUTRITION PER SERVE
Protein 5 g; Fat 25 g; Carbohydrate 15 g;
Dietary Fibre 2 g; Cholesterol 90 mg;
1235 kJ (295 cal)

COOK'S FILE

Note: If light soy sauce is not available, use half soy sauce and half water. Pickled ginger is available from Asian supermarkets.
Hint: Use scissors to cut the nori.

Peel the daikon radish and cut it into fine slices using a sharp knife.

Add 1 tablespoon water and the nori to the lightly beaten eggs.

Once the omelette has cooled, slice it into thin strips.

33

WARM RADICCHIO SALAD WITH CRUSHED TOMATO VINAIGRETTE

Preparation time: 40 minutes
Total cooking time: 25 minutes
Serves 4

1/4 cup (60 ml/2 fl oz) oil
6 cloves garlic, thinly sliced
1–2 tablespoons olive oil
7 egg tomatoes, cored and halved
1/4 cup (60 ml/2 fl oz) extra virgin olive oil
2 tablespoons red wine vinegar
1 teaspoon honey
920 g (1 lb 14 oz) chicory

1 onion, halved and sliced
1 radicchio lettuce

1 Heat the oil in a small pan, add the garlic and fry over moderately high heat for a few minutes, or until lightly browned. Drain on paper towels.
2 Heat a little of the olive oil in a frying pan and cook the tomatoes, cut-side-down, over moderate heat until browned and very soft. Turn to brown the other side. Transfer to a bowl to cool, then peel and discard the skins. Coarsely mash the flesh with a fork.
3 To make the vinaigrette, whisk about half of the crushed tomatoes, the extra virgin olive oil, vinegar and honey until combined. Season with salt and freshly ground black pepper.

4 Trim the coarse stems from the chicory, wash the leaves very well and drain. Cut into short lengths. Heat a little more olive oil in the frying pan, add the onion and cook until transparent. Add the chicory and stir until just wilted. Add the remaining tomatoes and stir until well combined. Season with salt and black pepper.
5 Tear any large radicchio leaves into smaller pieces. Toss through the chicory mixture. Transfer to a large serving bowl, drizzle with the tomato vinaigrette and sprinkle with the garlic. Serve immediately.

NUTRITION PER SERVE
Protein 7 g; Fat 35 g; Carbohydrate 9 g;
Dietary Fibre 8 g; Cholesterol 0 mg;
1620 kJ (385 cal)

Fry the garlic in the oil over moderate heat until lightly browned.

Cook the tomatoes until they are browned and very soft.

Tear any large radicchio leaves into smaller pieces.

BOK CHOY SALAD

Preparation time: 20 minutes
Total cooking time: 5 minutes
Serves 4

1 cup (250 ml/8 fl oz) chicken
   stock
1 small carrot, cut into julienne
   strips (see Note)
4 baby bok choy
100 g (3¼ oz) snow peas, thinly
   sliced
1 cup (90 g/3 oz) bean sprouts,
   trimmed
1 tablespoon chopped coriander

Sesame Dressing
⅓ cup (80 ml/2¾ fl oz) peanut
   oil
1 teaspoon sesame oil
1 tablespoon white vinegar
1 tablespoon sesame seeds,
   toasted
2 teaspoons grated fresh ginger
2 teaspoons honey, warmed
1 clove garlic, crushed

1 Pour the chicken stock into a frying pan and bring to the boil. Add the carrot and bok choy, cover and cook for 2 minutes. Drain the vegetables and leave to cool, then halve the bok choy lengthways.
2 To make the dressing, put the oils, vinegar, sesame seeds, ginger, honey and garlic in a small bowl and whisk to combine. Season with salt and pepper, to taste.
3 Place the cooled carrot strips and halved bok choy in a large serving dish and arrange the snow peas, bean sprouts and chopped coriander on top. Drizzle with the sesame dressing and serve immediately.

NUTRITION PER SERVE
Protein 7 g; Fat 20 g; Carbohydrate 10 g; Dietary Fibre 4 g; Cholesterol 0 mg; 1110 kJ (265 cal)

COOK'S FILE

Hint: To toast the sesame seeds, place in a dry pan and shake gently over medium heat until the seeds smell fragrant and begin to turn a pale golden colour. Turn the seeds out onto a plate and leave to cool.
Note: Julienne strips are even-sized strips of vegetables, the size and shape of matchsticks. They require only a little cooking (often just blanching) and look very decorative.

Cut the carrots into julienne strips, the size and shape of matchsticks.

Remove and discard the scraggly ends from the bean sprouts.

Using a large sharp knife, halve the bok choy lengthways.

ORANGE POPPY SEED ROASTED VEGETABLES

Preparation time: 20 minutes
Total cooking time: 50 minutes
Serves 6–8

500 g (1 lb) new potatoes, halved
6 parsnips, peeled and quartered lengthways
500 g (1 lb) orange sweet potato, cut into large pieces
335 g (10¾ oz) baby carrots, with some of the tops left on

6 pickling onions, halved
⅓ cup (80 ml/2¾ fl oz) oil
2 tablespoons poppy seeds
200 g (6½ oz) triple cream Brie, thinly sliced

Orange Dressing
½ cup (125 ml/4 fl oz) orange juice
2 cloves garlic, crushed
1 tablespoon Dijon mustard
1 teaspoon white wine vinegar
1 teaspoon sesame oil

1 Preheat the oven to moderately hot 200°C (400°F/Gas 6). Place all the vegetables and the oil in a large deep baking dish. Toss the vegetables to coat with the oil. Bake for 50 minutes, or until the vegetables are crisp and tender, tossing every 15 minutes. Sprinkle with the poppy seeds.
2 To make the dressing, whisk the ingredients in a small jug to combine.
3 Pour the dressing over the warm vegetables and toss to coat. Transfer to a large bowl, top with the Brie and serve immediately, while still warm.

NUTRITION PER SERVE (8)
Protein 10 g; Fat 20 g; Carbohydrate 35 g; Dietary Fibre 6 g; Cholesterol 25 mg; 1510 kJ (360 cal)

Quarter the parsnips lengthways, and cut the sweet potato into large pieces.

Sprinkle the cooked vegetables with the poppy seeds.

Pour the dressing over the warm vegetables and toss to coat.

ASPARAGUS AND RED CAPSICUM SALAD

Preparation time: 20 minutes
Total cooking time: 15 minutes
Serves 4

Dressing
2 red capsicums
1/3 cup (80 ml/2³/4 fl oz) virgin olive oil
1 clove garlic, crushed
2 tablespoons lemon juice
2 tablespoons chopped basil
2 tablespoons pine nuts

310 g (10 oz) fresh asparagus
small black olives

1 To make the dressing, cut the capsicums into large pieces, removing the seeds and white membrane. Place, skin-side-up, under a hot grill until the skin blackens and blisters. Cool under a tea towel or in a plastic bag, then carefully peel away and discard the skin. Finely dice the flesh.
2 Place the olive oil, garlic, lemon juice and basil in a small bowl and whisk to combine. Add the capsicum and pine nuts, and season with salt and pepper.

3 Trim and discard the woody ends from the asparagus. Plunge the asparagus into a large frying pan of boiling water and cook for 3 minutes, or until just tender. Drain and plunge into a bowl of iced water, then drain again and gently pat dry with paper towels. Arrange the asparagus on a large serving platter and spoon the dressing over the top. Garnish with the black olives. Delicious served with lemon wedges.

NUTRITION PER SERVE
Protein 4 g; Fat 25 g; Carbohydrate 5 g; Dietary Fibre 3 g; Cholesterol 0 mg; 1100 kJ (260 cal)

Grill the capsicum pieces until the skin blackens and blisters.

Add the diced capsicum and pine nuts to the other dressing ingredients.

Pat the cooked asparagus spears dry with paper towels.

ROAST BEETROOT AND ONION WEDGE SALAD

Preparation time: 30 minutes
Total cooking time: 1 hour 30 minutes
Serves 4–6

4 medium beetroots
3 red onions
1/3 cup (80 ml/2³/4 fl oz) oil
20 g (³/4 oz) butter
1 teaspoon ground cumin
1 teaspoon soft brown sugar
2 tablespoons orange juice
2 tablespoons orange zest
chopped chives, to garnish

Sour Cream Dressing
150 g (5 oz) sour cream
2 tablespoons chopped chives
1 tablespoon chopped thyme
1 teaspoon lemon juice

1 Preheat the oven to moderate 180°C (350°F/Gas 4). Trim the leafy tops from the beetroot, leaving a 4 cm (1½ inch) stalk, and wash thoroughly. Keep the beetroot whole to avoid bleeding during baking. Cut each onion into 6 large wedges, leaving the bases intact as much as possible so the wedges hold together. Put the oil in a large baking dish and add the beetroot and onion wedges. Bake for 1 hour 15 minutes. Remove the beetroot and onion onto separate plates and set aside to cool slightly. Peel and discard the skins from the beetroot. Trim the tops and tails to neaten, and cut into large wedges.
2 Heat the butter in a frying pan, add the cumin and brown sugar, and cook for 1 minute. Add the orange juice and simmer for 5 minutes, or until the juice has reduced slightly. Add the baked beetroot wedges and orange zest, and stir gently over low heat for 2 minutes.
3 To make the dressing, combine the sour cream, chopped chives, thyme and lemon juice. Arrange the cooked beetroot and onion wedges on a large serving plate and serve with the dressing. Sprinkle with the chopped chives to garnish.

NUTRITION PER SERVE (6)
Protein 3 g; Fat 25 g; Carbohydrate 10 g; Dietary Fibre 4 g; Cholesterol 40 mg; 1185 kJ (280 cal)

Trim the leafy tops from the beetroots, leaving a short stalk.

Cut the onions into wedges, leaving as much of the base intact as possible.

Add the beetroot wedges and orange zest to the pan.

MARINATED TOFU AND CARROT SESAME SALAD

Preparation time: 30 minutes
+ 1 hour marinating
Total cooking time: 15 minutes
Serves 4

500 g (1 lb) firm tofu
2 tablespoons grated fresh
    ginger
2 spring onions, finely sliced
1 tablespoon mirin
1/4 cup (60 ml/2 fl oz) soy sauce
1 teaspoon sesame oil
oil, for cooking
2 Lebanese cucumbers
2 carrots, peeled
1/4 Chinese cabbage, shredded
100 g (3 1/4 oz) crispy fried egg
    noodles
50 g (1 3/4 oz) roasted peanuts,
    roughly chopped
mint leaves, to garnish

Dressing
1 tablespoon grated lime rind
1 tablespoon sugar
2 tablespoons lime juice
1/4 cup (60 ml/2 fl oz) olive oil
2 tablespoons shredded mint
    leaves

1 Cut the tofu into 1 cm (1/2 inch) thick triangles. Put in a shallow dish with the ginger, spring onion, mirin, soy sauce and sesame oil. Cover and refrigerate for 1 hour.
2 Heat 2 tablespoons of the oil in a large non-stick frying pan. Add the tofu and cook, in batches, over high heat until it is crisp and golden. Remove from the pan and drain on paper towels.
3 Using a sharp vegetable peeler, cut the cucumbers and carrots into paper-thin ribbons. Arrange the cabbage on a large platter and top with the cucumber, carrot and tofu.
4 To make the dressing, gently whisk the ingredients in a bowl to combine. Drizzle the dressing over the salad and sprinkle with the noodles and nuts. Garnish with the mint leaves and serve immediately.

NUTRITION PER SERVE
Protein 20 g; Fat 30 g; Carbohydrate 20 g; Dietary Fibre 5 g; Cholesterol 10 mg; 1690 kJ (400 cal)

Marinate the tofu in the ginger, spring onion, mirin, soy sauce and sesame oil.

Fry the marinated tofu in batches until crisp and golden.

Use a sharp vegetable peeler to cut the cucumbers and carrots into ribbons.

Side Salads

PARSNIP AND BEAN SALAD

Cut 270 g (8³/4 oz) parsnip into julienne strips. Cut 200 g (6¹/2 oz) green beans in half, then in half lengthways. Add the parsnip and beans to a pan of boiling water and simmer for 2 minutes, then drain and refresh under cold water. Pat dry with paper towels and arrange the parsnip and beans in a serving bowl.

Whisk ¹/3 cup (80 ml/2³/4 fl oz) light olive oil, ¹/2 teaspoon finely grated orange rind, 2 tablespoons orange juice, 2 teaspoons wholegrain mustard, ¹/2 teaspoon curry powder, 1 tablespoon chopped coriander, salt and pepper to taste in a jug until well combined. Pour over the vegetables and sprinkle with 2 tablespoons toasted slivered almonds. Serves 2–4

NUTRITION PER SERVE (4): Protein 4 g; Fat 25 g; Carbohydrate 9 g; Dietary Fibre 4 g; Cholesterol 0 mg; 1085 kJ (260 cal)

WILD RICE AND WALNUT SALAD

Thoroughly rinse 1¹/2 cups (285 g/9¹/4 oz) wild rice under cold water. Put in a pan and fill with water to come 2.5 cm (1 inch) above the surface of the rice. Bring to the boil and cook for 5 minutes. Remove from the heat, cover and leave for 1 hour. Drain well and place in a bowl with 6 chopped spring onions, ³/4 cup (90 g/3 oz) toasted walnut pieces and 1 tablespoon chopped flat-leaf parsley.

Whisk ¹/3 cup (80 ml/2³/4 fl oz) walnut oil, 1 tablespoon olive oil, 2 tablespoons white wine vinegar, 1 tablespoon soy sauce and 2 teaspoons warm honey until combined. Pour the dressing over the rice mixture and toss well. Serves 6

NUTRITION PER SERVE: Protein 6 g; Fat 25 g; Carbohydrate 40 g; Dietary Fibre 3 g; Cholesterol 0 mg; 1795 kJ (425 cal)

CUCUMBER AND HERB SALAD

Cut 3 Lebanese cucumbers in half lengthways and use a teaspoon to remove the seeds. Slice the cucumber thinly and place in a bowl with 2 tablespoons chopped mint, 1 tablespoon chopped chives, 2 teaspoons chopped dill, 1 tablespoon olive oil, 2 teaspoons white wine vinegar, ¹/2 cup (125 g/4 oz) plain yoghurt, salt and freshly ground black pepper. Mix until well combined, cover and refrigerate for 1 hour before serving. Serves 4

NUTRITION PER SERVE: Protein 2 g; Fat 6 g; Carbohydrate 3 g; Dietary Fibre 1 g; Cholesterol 5 mg; 310 kJ (75 cal)

From top: Parsnip and Bean Salad; Wild Rice and Walnut Salad; Cucumber and Herb Salad

SWEET POTATO SALAD

Preheat the oven to moderately hot 200°C (400°F/Gas 6). Peel 1 kg (2 lb) orange sweet potato and cut it into pieces. Place in a large baking dish and mix with 1/4 cup (60 ml/ 2 fl oz) olive oil, salt and pepper to taste. Bake for 35–40 minutes, or until tender, shaking the pan occasionally. Transfer the mixture to a bowl.

While the potatoes are baking, heat 1/4 cup (60 ml/2 fl oz) olive oil in a small pan and add 2 tablespoons sunflower seeds, 2 tablespoons pepitas (pumpkin seeds), 1 tablespoon poppy seeds and 1 tablespoon sesame seeds. Stir-fry until lightly golden. Allow to cool.

Whisk 2 tablespoons balsamic vinegar, 2 tablespoons chopped fresh coriander and 2 teaspoons tomato mustard until smooth. Pour the dressing over the sweet potato, add the seeds and toss well. Serves 4–6

NUTRITION PER SERVE (6): Protein 6 g; Fat 25 g; Carbohydrate 25 g; Dietary Fibre 4 g; Cholesterol 140 mg; 1460 kJ (345 cal)

CARROT AND SULTANA SALAD

Grate 3 carrots into a bowl. Add 1/2 cup (60 g/2 oz) coarsely chopped pecans or walnuts, 1/2 cup (60 g/2 oz) sultanas and 2 tablespoons chopped flat-leaf parsley.

Whisk together 1/4 cup (60 ml/2 fl oz) olive oil, 2 teaspoons honey, 1 1/2 tablespoons lemon juice, a pinch of ground cinnamon, salt and freshly ground black pepper to taste. Pour the dressing over the carrot mixture and toss well. For a different flavour add 1 teaspoon grated fresh ginger to the dressing. Serves 4

NUTRITION PER SERVE: Protein 3 g; Fat 25 g; Carbohydrate 20 g; Dietary Fibre 4 g; Cholesterol 0 mg; 1280 kJ (305 cal)

RISONI AND PISTACHIO PESTO SALAD

Add 250 g (8 oz) risoni pasta to a large pan of boiling salted water and cook until just tender. Drain, rinse under cold water and drain well. Place 1/3 cup (10 g/1/4 oz) celery leaves, 45 g (1 1/2 oz) rocket leaves, 1/2 cup (50 g/1 3/4 oz) freshly grated Parmesan, 2 tablespoons olive oil, 1 clove garlic and 1/4 cup (60 ml/2 fl oz) vegetable stock in a food processor. Process in short bursts until the mixture is fine and almost smooth. Add 1/3 cup (40 g/1 1/4 oz) chopped pistachio nuts and process in short bursts until combined. Combine the pistachio pesto with the pasta, add 1 finely diced small yellow capsicum and 2 tablespoons white wine vinegar. Stir until well combined. Season to taste with salt and freshly ground black pepper, cover the salad and refrigerate for 1 hour before serving. Serves 4–6

NUTRITION PER SERVE (6): Protein 10 g; Fat 15 g; Carbohydrate 30 g; Dietary Fibre 3 g; Cholesterol 8 mg; 1165 kJ (275 cal)

From top: Sweet Potato Salad; Carrot and Sultana Salad; Risoni and Pistachio Pesto Salad

SUMMER BREAD SALAD

Preparation time: 20 minutes
Total cooking time: 15 minutes
Serves 6–8

2 red capsicums
2 yellow capsicums
6 egg (Roma) tomatoes, cut into
    large chunks
100 g (3¼ oz) capers, drained
100 g (3¼ oz) anchovies, halved
100 g (3¼ oz) black olives
150 g (5 oz) bocconcini, halved
1 Italian wood-fired loaf
2 cups (60 g/2 oz) basil leaves

Dressing
4 cloves garlic, finely chopped
¼ cup (60 ml/2 fl oz) red wine
    vinegar
½ cup (125 ml/4 fl oz) extra
    virgin olive oil

1 Cut the capsicums into large pieces, removing the seeds and white membrane. Place, skin-side-up, under a hot grill, until the skin blackens and blisters. Cool in a plastic bag or under a tea towel, then peel away the skin and cut into thick strips.
2 Put the capsicum, tomato, capers, anchovies, olives and bocconcini in a bowl and toss to combine.

3 To make the dressing, put the ingredients in a screwtop jar and shake to combine.
4 Cut the bread into large pieces, and place in a serving bowl. Drizzle with the dressing and mix until the bread is coated. Add the capsicum mixture and basil leaves, and toss gently.

NUTRITION PER SERVE (8)
Protein 15 g; Fat 25 g; Carbohydrate 35 g; Dietary Fibre 4 g; Cholesterol 25 mg; 1870 kJ (445 cal)

COOK'S FILE

Note: This salad is based on the Tuscan favourite which uses leftover crusty bread to make a salad.

Put the grilled capsicum pieces in a plastic bag until cool enough to handle.

Combine the capsicum, tomato, capers, anchovies, olives and bocconcini.

Using a bread knife, cut the wood-fired loaf into large pieces.

CRUNCHY HALOUMI SALAD

Preparation time: 30 minutes
+ 2 hours marinating
Total cooking time: 20 minutes
Serves 6–8

2 red capsicums
300 g (10 oz) haloumi cheese
2 cloves garlic, crushed
1/4 teaspoon chilli flakes
1/4 cup (60 ml/2 fl oz) olive oil
2 teaspoons chopped marjoram
1 small loaf fig and walnut
    bread or fruit bread, thickly
    sliced
250 g (8 oz) watercress,
    trimmed
250 g (8 oz) pear tomatoes,
    halved
2 avocados, sliced
375 g (12 oz) smoked tuna
    slices or tuna in brine,
    drained

Dressing
2 tablespoons red wine vinegar
2 cloves garlic, crushed
1 teaspoon honey
1 tablespoon walnut oil
1/4 cup (60 ml/2 fl oz) olive oil

1 Cut the capsicums into large pieces, removing the seeds and membrane. Place, skin-side-up, under a hot grill until the skin blackens and blisters. Cool under a tea towel or in a plastic bag, then peel away the skin and slice into thick strips.
2 Cut the haloumi cheese into thick slices and place in a shallow dish. Combine the garlic, chilli flakes, olive oil and marjoram, and pour the mixture over the haloumi. Cover the dish and refrigerate for 2 hours. Drain, reserving the marinade.
3 Toast one side of the fig and walnut bread slices until golden brown. Turn over and place a slice of the marinated haloumi on the untoasted side. Grill under high heat until the cheese is golden brown. Arrange the watercress on individual serving plates or a large platter, and top with the tomato, avocado, capsicum and tuna. Cut the haloumi croutons in half and arrange around the edge of the salad.
4 To make the dressing, put the reserved marinade, red wine vinegar, crushed garlic, honey, walnut oil and olive oil in a bowl and whisk to combine. Drizzle over the salad and serve immediately.

NUTRITION PER SERVE (8)
Protein 30 g; Fat 35 g; Carbohydrate 40 g; Dietary Fibre 5 g; Cholesterol 45 mg; 2440 kJ (580 cal)

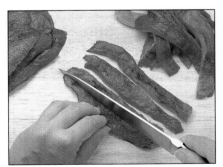

Slice the grilled, peeled capsicum into thick strips.

Pour the combined garlic, chilli, oil and marjoram over the haloumi.

Place a slice of marinated haloumi on one side of the bread slices.

ROAST SWEET POTATO AND CAPSICUM SALAD

Preparation time: 15 minutes
Total cooking time: 40 minutes
Serves 4

½ cup (125 ml/4 fl oz) olive oil
1 tablespoon chopped oregano
    or marjoram
1 clove garlic, crushed
3 red capsicums
500 g (1 lb) orange sweet potato
flaked sea salt
1 tablespoon balsamic vinegar
oregano leaves, to garnish

1 Preheat the oven to moderate 180°C (350°F/Gas 4). Place the oil, oregano or marjoram and garlic in a jug. Season with freshly ground black pepper and whisk with a small wire whisk or fork to combine.
2 Halve the capsicums lengthways and remove the seeds and white membrane. Cut the sweet potato lengthways into slices.
3 Brush the capsicum and sweet potato slices lightly with the herb oil mixture and place in a single layer on baking trays. Sprinkle lightly with the sea salt and bake for 40 minutes, or until the capsicum and sweet potato are tender and beginning to brown slightly on the edges. Leave the vegetables to cool, then arrange them on a serving platter.
4 Add the balsamic vinegar to the remaining oil mixture and drizzle over the salad. Serve sprinkled with the fresh oregano leaves.

NUTRITION PER SERVE
Protein 4 g; Fat 30 g; Carbohydrate 20 g; Dietary Fibre 3 g; Cholesterol 0 mg; 1520 kJ (360 cal)

Combine the oil, oregano or marjoram, and garlic in a small jug.

Cut the capsicums in half lengthways, and cut the sweet potato into long slices.

Brush the capsicum and sweet potato with the oil mixture and bake until tender.

BROCCOLI SALAD

Preparation time: 15 minutes
Total cooking time: 15 minutes
Serves 4

6 eggs, at room temperature
    (see Note)
500 g (1 lb) broccoli
1 tablespoon olive oil
7 spring onions, sliced
3 thin slices prosciutto, cut into
    strips
2 tablespoons pine nuts,
    toasted

Dressing
¼ cup (60 ml/2 fl oz) olive oil
1 tablespoon balsamic vinegar
1 teaspoon Dijon mustard

1 Cook the eggs in simmering water for 6–7 minutes (so the yolks will be set but not too firm). Drain and cover with cold water. When cool, peel away the shells and cut each egg in half.
2 Cut the broccoli into single stalks and cook in a pan of boiling water for 3 minutes. Drain and cool under gently running cold water. Drain and pat dry with paper towels. Arrange in a shallow serving dish.

3 To make the dressing, whisk the ingredients in a small bowl to combine. Season with salt and pepper.
4 Heat the oil in a pan, cook the spring onion until soft and spoon over the broccoli. Arrange the egg on top, scatter with the prosciutto and pine nuts, and drizzle with the dressing.

NUTRITION PER SERVE
Protein 20 g; Fat 35 g; Carbohydrate 2 g; Dietary Fibre 6 g; Cholesterol 280 mg; 1590 kJ (380 cal)

COOK'S FILE

Note: Eggs at room temperature are less likely to crack during cooking.

Using a sharp knife, cut the cooled, peeled eggs in half.

Separate the broccoli into single stalks before cooking.

Cook the spring onion in the heated oil until it is soft.

MISTY MUSHROOM SALAD

Preparation time: 15 minutes
Total cooking time: Nil
Serves 4

Dressing
1/2 cup (125 g/4 oz) plain
    yoghurt
1/2 cup (125 g/4 oz) mayonnaise
75 g (2 1/2 oz) creamy or mild
    blue cheese
2 tablespoons cream

500 g (1 lb) button mushrooms
2 celery sticks, sliced
2 tablespoons chopped chives
35 g (1 1/4 oz) rocket leaves
2 tablespoons chopped walnuts

1 To make the dressing, put the yoghurt, mayonnaise, cheese and cream in a food processor and process until smooth. Season with salt and pepper, to taste.
2 Wipe the mushrooms with a dry paper towel, cut each in half and place in a large bowl with the celery and half the chives. Add the dressing and toss the salad gently to combine.
3 Arrange the rocket leaves in a large serving dish and spoon in the mushroom and celery mixture. Sprinkle with the chopped walnuts and reserved chives.

NUTRITION PER SERVE
Protein 10 g; Fat 25 g; Carbohydrate 10 g; Dietary Fibre 4 g; Cholesterol 45 mg; 1295 kJ (310 cal)

COOK'S FILE

Note: This salad can be prepared up to 2 hours ahead and stored, covered, in the refrigerator.

Blend the dressing ingredients in a food processor until smooth.

Clean the mushrooms by wiping gently with a dry paper towel.

Add the dressing to the mushrooms, celery, and chives and toss gently.

GAZPACHO SALAD

Preparation time: 25 minutes
Total cooking time: 10 minutes
Serves 4–6

3 thick slices white bread,
   crusts removed and cubed
2 tablespoons olive oil
4 egg (Roma) tomatoes, chopped
2 Lebanese cucumbers, chopped
1 large red capsicum, chopped
1 large green capsicum, chopped
1 red onion, sliced

¹/₂ cup (100 g/3¹/₄ oz) fresh or
   frozen corn kernels, cooked
¹/₂ cup (60 g/2 oz) medium
   black olives, pitted

Dressing
¹/₂ cup (125 ml/4 fl oz) olive oil
1 clove garlic, crushed
2 tablespoons red wine vinegar
2 tablespoons shredded basil

1 Preheat the oven to moderate 180°C (350°F/Gas 4). Put the bread in a bowl, add the oil and toss quickly until absorbed. Bake the bread in a single layer on a baking tray for 10 minutes, or until golden. Allow to cool.

2 To make the dressing, whisk the ingredients in a bowl until combined. Season with salt and pepper.

3 Place the tomato, cucumber, capsicum, onion, corn and olives in a large bowl. Add the dressing and toss gently to combine. Place the salad in a serving dish and scatter the croutons on top. Serve immediately.

NUTRITION PER SERVE (6)
Protein 4 g; Fat 30 g; Carbohydrate 10 g;
Dietary Fibre 4 g; Cholesterol 0 mg;
1320 kJ (315 cal)

Toss the bread cubes in the oil until the oil is absorbed.

Bake the bread cubes on a baking tray in a single layer until golden.

Combine the tomato, cucumber, capsicum, onion, corn and olives.

WARM WILD MUSHROOM SALAD

Preparation time: 15 minutes
Total cooking time: 15 minutes
Serves 4

100 g (3¼ oz) hazelnuts
1 mizuna lettuce
85 g (2¾ oz) baby curly endive
40 g (1¼ oz) baby English
    spinach leaves
2 tablespoons hazelnut oil
2 tablespoons light olive oil
500 g (1 lb) wild mushrooms
    (enoki, shimeji, Shiitake,
    oyster)
150 g (5 oz) strong blue cheese,
    crumbled

Tomato Mustard Vinaigrette
½ cup (125 ml/4 fl oz) light
    olive oil
2 tablespoons tarragon vinegar
1 teaspoon tomato mustard

1 Preheat the oven to moderate 180°C (350°F/Gas 4). Put the hazelnuts on a baking tray and cook for 10 minutes, shaking the tray occasionally. Remove from the oven, cool, and remove the skins by rubbing the nuts together in a tea towel. Coarsely chop the nuts.
2 Remove the tough lower stems from the mizuna and endive, and tear the larger leaves into bite-sized pieces. Wash the mizuna, endive and spinach under cold water, dry completely and refrigerate until well chilled.
3 To make the vinaigrette, whisk the ingredients together and season to taste with salt and freshly ground black pepper.
4 Heat the oils in a medium frying pan. Add the mushrooms and sauté

for 3–4 minutes, or until they just begin to soften. Remove from the heat, allow to cool slightly, then stir in the vinaigrette. Arrange the salad greens on individual serving plates. Spoon the mushrooms over the top and sprinkle each with the cheese, hazelnuts and some freshly ground black pepper. Serve with cornbread.

NUTRITION PER SERVE
Protein 10 g; Fat 75 g; Carbohydrate 20 g; Dietary Fibre 4 g; Cholesterol 40 mg; 3375 kJ (805 cal)

COOK'S FILE

Note: Chestnut mushrooms or chanterelles can also be used. Pink oyster mushrooms, if available, give a good colour contrast to this dish.

Rub the hazelnuts together in a tea towel to remove the skins.

Remove the tough lower stems from the baby curly endive.

Sauté the mushrooms until they just begin to soften.

FENNEL AND ANCHOVY SALAD

Preparation time: 15 minutes
Total cooking time: 10 minutes
Serves 4–6

4 egg (Roma) tomatoes
3 fennel bulbs
5 cups (1.25 litres) chicken
    stock
2 tablespoons finely chopped
    flat-leaf parsley
12 black olives
8 anchovy fillets

Dressing
1/3 cup (80 ml/2³/4 fl oz) olive oil
2 tablespoons lemon juice
1 clove garlic, crushed

1 Score a cross in the base of each tomato. Place in a heatproof bowl and cover with boiling water. Leave for 1 minute, then drain and peel away the skin. Halve the tomatoes, scoop out the seeds and chop the flesh.
2 Cut the fennel bulbs into quarters, keeping the root end intact. Bring the chicken stock to the boil, add the fennel and simmer, covered, for 5 minutes. Drain the fennel, reserving the stock, and place in a serving dish.
3 To make the dressing, whisk the oil, lemon juice and garlic with 2 tablespoons of the reserved stock. Season with salt and pepper.
4 Spoon the dressing over the fennel and leave to cool to room temperature. Scatter the parsley, tomato, olives and anchovies over the top and serve.

NUTRITION PER SERVE (6)
Protein 3 g; Fat 15 g; Carbohydrate 2 g; Dietary Fibre 1 g; Cholesterol 6 mg; 680 kJ (160 cal)

Using a sharp knife, finely chop the flat-leaf parsley.

Peel away the skin of the tomatoes, starting at the base.

Cut the tomatoes in half and scoop out the seeds with a teaspoon.

BROAD BEAN AND EGGPLANT SALAD WITH GARLIC CROUTONS

Preparation time: 30 minutes
Total cooking time: 30 minutes
Serves 4

350 g (11¼ oz) slender
    eggplant, diagonally sliced
1 teaspoon salt
500 g (1 lb) fresh broad beans,
    shelled, or 250 g (8 oz)
    frozen shelled beans
155 g (5 oz) fresh asparagus,
    cut into short lengths
⅓ cup (80 ml/2¾ fl oz) extra
    virgin olive oil
1 clove garlic, crushed
3 slices pumpkin or corn bread,
    or 1 large bread roll, cut into
    small cubes
¼ small yellow capsicum, finely
    sliced
3 spring onions, finely chopped
6–8 torn red oakleaf lettuce
    leaves
1 cup (30 g/1 oz) watercress
2 tablespoons finely sliced opal
    or green basil leaves
2 tablespoons toasted pistachio
    nuts, coarsely chopped

Dressing
⅓ cup (80 ml/2¾ fl oz) extra
    virgin olive oil
2 tablespoons balsamic vinegar

1 Preheat the oven to moderately hot 200°C (400°F/Gas 6). Toss the eggplant with the salt and place in a colander. Set aside to drain.
2 Cook the broad beans in a large pan of boiling water for 5 minutes (3 minutes if using frozen beans), and transfer to a bowl of cold water. When cool, peel and discard the skins. Plunge the asparagus into the boiling water and cook for 2 minutes, then drain and rinse under cold water.
3 Heat the olive oil in a small pan over low heat, add the garlic and sauté for 1 minute. Shake the eggplant slices dry but do not rinse. Place in a single layer on a baking tray, brush lightly with the garlic oil and bake for 10 minutes.
4 Toss the bread cubes lightly in 1 tablespoon of the garlic oil. Spread

on a baking tray. When the eggplant has baked for 10 minutes, turn the slices over and brush with the remaining garlic oil. Return to the oven along with the croutons. Reduce the temperature to moderate 180°C (350°F/Gas 4) and bake for 10 minutes, or until the croutons are golden and the eggplant is tender. Remove and cool on the trays.
5 To make the dressing, put the oil and vinegar in a small bowl, season

with salt and freshly ground black pepper, and mix well.
6 Place the eggplant, broad beans, asparagus, croutons, capsicum, spring onion, lettuce, watercress and basil in a serving bowl. Pour in the dressing and toss lightly. Scatter with the pistachios before serving.

NUTRITION PER SERVE
Protein 20 g; Fat 45 g; Carbohydrate 25 g; Dietary Fibre 20 g; Cholesterol 0 mg; 2315 kJ (550 cal)

Sprinkle the eggplant with the salt and leave to drain in a colander.

When the broad beans are cool, peel away and discard the skins.

CHILLI CUCUMBER AND MUNG BEAN SALAD

Preparation time: 20 minutes
Total cooking time: 5 minutes
Serves 4

Dressing
1/4 cup (60 ml/2 fl oz) oil
2 teaspoons black mustard
  seeds
1 teaspoon black sesame seeds
1/2 teaspoon ground cumin
1 1/2 teaspoons turmeric
1 small red chilli, finely
  chopped
1/2 cup (125 g/4 oz) plain
  yoghurt

100 g (3 1/4 oz) carrot, grated
200 g (6 1/2 oz) mung bean
  sprouts
3 Lebanese cucumbers,
  quartered lengthwise, then
  sliced
1/2 cup (30 g/1 oz) shredded
  coconut
1/2 cup (25 g/3/4 oz) chopped
  coriander
2 tablespoons shredded kaffir
  lime leaves
sprig of coriander, to garnish

1 To make the dressing, heat the oil in a small pan and add the mustard seeds. Cook, stirring, over low heat until the seeds pop. Add the sesame seeds and stir for 10–15 seconds, then add the ground cumin, turmeric and chilli. Stir for a further 10–15 seconds. Remove from the heat, add the yoghurt and mix well.

2 Put the carrot, sprouts, cucumber, coconut, coriander and half the lime leaves in a bowl and toss lightly. Add the dressing and toss until evenly coated. Sprinkle with the remaining lime leaves and a sprig of coriander.

NUTRITION PER SERVE
Protein 5 g; Fat 20 g; Carbohydrate 6 g;
Dietary Fibre 5 g; Cholesterol 5 mg;
1010 kJ (240 cal)

COOK'S FILE

Note: Mustard seeds are available in black or yellow. The black seeds have a more pungent aroma and taste.

Fry the mustard seeds in the oil until the seeds pop.

Stir the yoghurt into the seeds, cumin, turmeric and chilli, and mix well.

Add half the shredded kaffir lime leaves to the salad and toss lightly.

ORANGE AND FENNEL SALAD

Preparation time: 15 minutes
Total cooking time: Nil
Serves 4

3 oranges, peeled and sliced
2 baby fennel bulbs, thinly
    sliced
1 large avocado, sliced
100 g (3¼ oz) rocket leaves
2 tablespoons pine nuts

Dressing
2 tablespoons orange juice
1 teaspoon Dijon mustard
¼ teaspoon ground cumin
⅓ cup (80 ml/2¾ fl oz) extra
    virgin olive oil

1 Layer the orange slices, fennel, avocado and rocket leaves on a serving platter.
2 To make the dressing, whisk together the orange juice, mustard, cumin and olive oil. Season to taste with salt and pepper.
3 Drizzle the dressing over the salad and top with the pine nuts.

NUTRITION PER SERVE
Protein 5 g; Fat 40 g; Carbohydrate 15 g; Dietary Fibre 9 g; Cholesterol 0 mg; 1745 kJ (415 cal)

COOK'S FILE

Variation: Blood oranges may be used instead of regular oranges in this recipe. They look lovely and will give the salad a sweet, tart flavour. Blood oranges are only in season for a very short period of time. The orange juice in the dressing works in the same way as lemon juice and will prevent the avocado from browning.

Thinly slice the fennel bulbs, discarding the green tops.

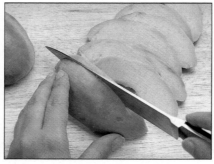

Peel the avocado and remove the seed, then cut into thin slices.

Put the orange juice, mustard and cumin in a small bowl, and add the olive oil.

PAPAYA AND GORGONZOLA SALAD

Preparation time: 20 minutes
Total cooking time: 20 minutes
Serves 4

1 cup (250 ml/8 fl oz) orange
    juice
1 tablespoon oil
1 tablespoon soft brown sugar
1 fennel bulb, sliced
2 heads witlof, quartered
250 g (8 oz) watercress, ends
    trimmed
1 papaya, sliced
200 g (6¹/2 oz) Gorgonzola
    cheese, crumbled
¹/2 cup (70 g/2¹/4 oz) hazelnuts,
    roughly chopped

Dressing
1 cup (30 g/1 oz) loosely packed
    basil leaves
¹/2 cup (125 ml/4 fl oz) olive oil

1 Put the orange juice in a frying pan
and cook over high heat until reduced
by a third.
2 Stir the oil and brown sugar in a
frying pan over low heat until the
sugar dissolves. Add the fennel, witlof
and orange juice, cover and cook for
15 minutes, or until the vegetables
have caramelised. Check the liquid a
couple of times during cooking; if it is
looking too dry add a little water.
3 Divide the watercress among
four serving plates, top with the
papaya, caramelised vegetables,
Gorgonzola and hazelnuts.
4 To make the dressing, process the
basil and oil in a food processor until
combined, then strain and drizzle over
the salad.

NUTRITION PER SERVE
Protein 15 g; Fat 60 g; Carbohydrate 20 g;
Dietary Fibre 10 g; Cholesterol 50 mg;
2885 kJ (685 cal)

COOK'S FILE

Note: Gorgonzola is a blue-veined
cheese with a strong, sharp flavour. It
is named after the Italian town where
it originated, and is made from
pressed cows milk. If Gorgonzola
cheese is not available, you can
substitute Roquefort or Blue Castello
in this recipe.

*Using a large sharp knife, cut the fennel
bulb into slices.*

*Cut the papaya in half, scrape out the
seeds and slice the flesh.*

*Cook the orange juice over high heat
until it is reduced by a third.*

*Add the fennel and witlof to the oil and
sugar mixture.*

MEAT & POULTRY

SMOKED CHICKEN CAESAR SALAD

Preparation time: 25 minutes
Total cooking time: 15 minutes
Serves 4

Garlic Croutons
1 thin baguette
45 g (1½ oz) unsalted butter
½ cup (125 ml/4 fl oz) olive
   oil
4 cloves garlic, crushed

1 cos lettuce, tough outer leaves
   discarded
1 large smoked chicken (about
   950 g/1 lb 14 oz)
1½ cups (150 g/5 oz) Parmesan
   shavings

Dressing
2 eggs
2 cloves garlic, crushed
2 tablespoons lemon juice
2 teaspoons Dijon mustard
45 g (1½ oz) can anchovy
   fillets, drained
1 cup (250 ml/8 fl oz) olive
   oil
¼ teaspoon salt
1 teaspoon freshly ground black
   pepper

1 To make the garlic croutons, slice the baguette diagonally into 1 cm (½ inch) thick slices. Melt the butter and olive oil in a large frying pan over moderate heat. Stir in the crushed garlic. Fry the bread slices, a few at a time, until golden. Remove from the pan and drain on paper towels.
2 Separate the lettuce leaves, wash and dry thoroughly. Tear the larger leaves into pieces and refrigerate until well chilled. Cut the chicken meat into bite-sized chunks. Refrigerate while preparing the dressing.
3 To make the dressing, blend or process the eggs, garlic, lemon juice, mustard and anchovies. With the motor running, gradually pour in the oil in a thin stream and process until thick. Season with the salt and pepper.
4 In a large bowl, combine the torn lettuce leaves, chicken, about half of the croutons and half the Parmesan. Add the dressing and toss well. Arrange 2–3 whole leaves in each individual serving bowl, spoon in the salad and sprinkle with the remaining croutons and Parmesan. Season liberally with freshly ground black pepper and serve immediately.

NUTRITION PER SERVE
Protein 45 g; Fat 120 g; Carbohydrate 10 g; Dietary Fibre 2 g; Cholesterol 235 mg; 5350 kJ (1275 cal)

Roughly chop the smoked chicken into bite-sized chunks.

Process the eggs, garlic, lemon juice, mustard and anchovies.

INDIAN-STYLE LAMB COUSCOUS SALAD

Preparation time: 25 minutes
Total cooking time: 35 minutes
Serves 4–6

250 g (8 oz) lamb backstrap
    (tender eye of the lamb loin)
1 tablespoon mild curry powder
2 tablespoons pepitas (pumpkin
    seeds)
2 tablespoons sesame seeds
2 teaspoons cumin seeds
2 teaspoons coriander seeds
1 tablespoon oil
2 tablespoons lemon juice
1 onion, chopped
1 carrot, chopped
125 g (4 oz) orange sweet
    potato, cubed
1 clove garlic, finely chopped
2 teaspoons oil, extra
1 cup (185 g/6 oz) couscous
1/4 cup (50 g/13/4 oz) raisins

1 Sprinkle the lamb with the combined curry powder and a pinch of salt, then turn to coat well. Cover with plastic wrap and refrigerate while preparing the salad.
2 Place the pepitas and sesame seeds in a dry frying pan and cook, stirring, over medium-high heat until the seeds begin to brown. Add the cumin and coriander seeds and continue stirring until the pepitas are puffed and begin to pop. Remove from the heat and allow to cool.
3 Heat the oil in a pan, add the lamb and cook over medium-high heat for 5–8 minutes, or until browned and tender. Remove from the pan, drizzle with half the lemon juice and leave to cool to room temperature. Turn the

meat occasionally to coat in the lemon juice while cooling. To the same pan, add the onion, carrot and sweet potato and stir over high heat until the onion is translucent. Reduce the heat to medium, add 1/4 cup (60 ml/2 fl oz) water, cover and cook for about 3 minutes, or until the vegetables are tender. Stir in the chopped garlic and remaining lemon juice.
4 Pour 1 cup (250 ml/8 fl oz) boiling water into a heatproof bowl and add the extra oil. Add the couscous and stir until combined. Leave for about 2 minutes, or until the water has been

absorbed. Fluff gently with a fork to separate the grains. Add the vegetable mixture, raisins and most of the toasted nuts and seeds, reserving some to sprinkle over the top, and toss until just combined. Spoon the mixture onto a serving plate. Slice the lamb thinly and arrange over the salad. Drizzle with any leftover lemon juice and sprinkle with the reserved nuts and seeds.

NUTRITION PER SERVE (6)
Protein 15 g; Fat 10 g; Carbohydrate 30 g; Dietary Fibre 3 g; Cholesterol 30 mg; 1135 kJ (270 cal)

Sprinkle the lamb backstrap with the combined curry powder and salt.

Fry the seeds in a dry frying pan until the pepitas puff up.

When the water has been absorbed, fluff the couscous gently with a fork.

CORONATION CHICKEN

Preparation time: 20 minutes
Total cooking time: 30 minutes
Serves 4

4 chicken breast fillets
1 carrot, chopped
1 celery stick, chopped
1/2 small onion, chopped
4 whole peppercorns
1 bay leaf
1 tablespoon oil
1 onion, chopped
2 teaspoons curry powder
1 large tomato, peeled, seeded
    and finely chopped
1/2 cup (125 ml/4 fl oz) dry
    white wine
2 teaspoons tomato paste
1/2 cup (125 g/4 oz) thick plain
    yoghurt
1/2 cup (125 g/4 oz) mayonnaise
2 teaspoons lemon juice
2 tablespoons mango chutney

1 Place the chicken, carrot, celery, onion, peppercorns and bay leaf in a single layer in a large frying pan. Add enough water to just cover the chicken. Bring to the boil, reduce the heat and simmer for 8 minutes, or until the chicken is tender. Leave to cool in the liquid then remove and slice the chicken into thin strips.
2 Heat the oil in a frying pan and add the onion and curry powder. Cook, stirring, for a few minutes, or until the onion is translucent. Add the chopped tomato and wine, bring to the boil, then reduce the heat and simmer for 10 minutes.
3 Stir in the tomato paste, yoghurt, mayonnaise, lemon juice and mango chutney. Mix until well combined and season with salt and freshly ground black pepper. Add the chicken strips and mix well. This dish looks lovely served on a bed of salad greens.

NUTRITION PER SERVE
Protein 30 g; Fat 20 g; Carbohydrate 15 g; Dietary Fibre 3 g; Cholesterol 70 mg; 1570 kJ (375 cal)

COOK'S FILE

Note: Coronation chicken is an English favourite and although traditionally served with a rice salad, it also makes a great sandwich filling. Use any variety of breads or crackers with some snow pea sprouts or salad greens to garnish.

Peel the tomato, remove the seeds, and finely chop the flesh.

Cover the chicken, carrot, celery, onion, peppercorns and bay leaf with water.

Stir in the tomato paste, yoghurt, mayonnaise, lemon juice and chutney.

CRISP NOODLE, PORK AND SHREDDED VEGETABLE SALAD

Preparation time: 25 minutes
Total cooking time: 40 minutes
Serves 4–6

1 teaspoon paprika
2 teaspoons ground coriander
3 teaspoons ground cumin
350 g (11¼ oz) pork fillets
2 tablespoons oil
oil, for deep-frying
75 g (2½ oz) rice vermicelli
100 g (3¼ oz) daikon radish, peeled
1 green mango, cut into thin strips
100 g (3¼ oz) bean sprouts, trimmed
2 tablespoons toasted sesame seeds
1 small mild green chilli, cut into thin strips
¼ cup (15 g/½ oz) chopped Vietnamese mint
½ cup (15 g/½ oz) loosely packed watercress

Dressing
⅓ cup (80 ml/2¾ fl oz) peanut oil
1 teaspoon sesame oil
2 teaspoons lime juice
1 teaspoon finely chopped ginger
1 tablespoon rice vinegar
2 teaspoons fish sauce
1 teaspoon wasabi paste

1 Combine the paprika, coriander and cumin in a bowl. Add the pork fillets and coat with the mixture. Heat the 2 tablespoons of oil in a large pan, add the pork and cook over medium heat for 25–30 minutes, or until well browned and just cooked. Set aside to cool completely.

2 Heat the oil for deep-frying. When the oil is ready a small piece of vermicelli should puff up immediately when added. Use a pair of tongs to add the vermicelli to the hot oil, in batches. Use the tongs to separate the noodles once they start to puff so that they cook evenly. As soon as they are puffed and crisp, remove from the oil with the tongs. Drain on paper towels.

3 Slice the radish into fine strips using a vegetable peeler and place in a large bowl. Add the strips of mango, bean sprouts, sesame seeds, chilli, mint and watercress. Toss lightly to combine. Slice the pork thinly and add it to the salad. Add the fried noodles and toss gently.

4 To make the dressing, combine all the ingredients and mix well. Season with freshly ground black pepper, then pour over the salad and serve.

NUTRITION PER SERVE (6)
Protein 15 g; Fat 25 g; Carbohydrate 7 g; Dietary Fibre 2 g; Cholesterol 35 mg; 1295 kJ (310 cal)

COOK'S FILE

Note: The pork can be cooked up to 24 hours in advance and stored in the refrigerator. It is much easier to slice thinly if chilled first. Rice vermicelli can be purchased in straight noodles, in sticks, or tightly packed together.

Cut the green chilli into thin strips, wearing a glove to protect your hand.

Cook the rice vermicelli until it is puffed and crisp.

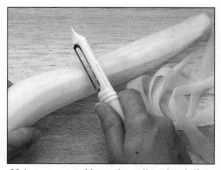
Using a vegetable peeler, slice the daikon radish into fine strips.

LAMB SALAD WITH HUMMUS DRESSING

Preparation time: 20 minutes
Total cooking time: 25 minutes
Serves 4

2 tablespoons olive oil
250 g (8 oz) lamb fillets
250 g (8 oz) slender eggplant
1 red capsicum, quartered
1 green or yellow capsicum, quartered
1/4 cup (7 g/1/4 oz) flat-leaf parsley leaves

Hummus Dressing
1/4 cup (60 ml/2 fl oz) lemon juice
1/4 cup (60 ml/2 fl oz) olive oil
1 teaspoon sugar
1 tablespoon hummus

1 Heat half the oil in a pan, add the lamb and cook until browned all over and still pink in the centre. Remove and drain on paper towels.
2 Halve the eggplant lengthways (if they are thick, cut each into 3–4 long slices). Lightly brush the eggplant and capsicum with the remaining oil. Cook under a hot grill until the eggplant is brown and tender and the capsicum is blackened and blistered. Cool the capsicum under a tea towel or in a plastic bag, then peel away the skin and cut the flesh into thick strips.
3 To make the dressing, whisk the ingredients in a jug until smooth.
4 Slice the lamb diagonally into long thin strips. Combine with the eggplant, capsicum and parsley in a bowl, then pile onto serving plates. Drizzle with the dressing just before serving.

NUTRITION PER SERVE
Protein 15 g; Fat 25 g; Carbohydrate 5 g; Dietary Fibre 2 g; Cholesterol 40 mg; 1355 kJ (320 cal)

Lightly brush the eggplant and capsicum with the remaining olive oil.

Slice the grilled, peeled capsicum into thick strips.

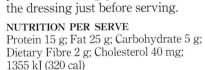

Whisk the lemon juice, olive oil, sugar and hummus together until smooth.

PACIFIC CHICKEN SALAD

Preparation time: 20 minutes
Total cooking time: 15 minutes
Serves 4

1 cup (250 ml/8 fl oz) coconut
   milk
1 tablespoon nam pla (Thai fish
   sauce)
1 tablespoon grated palm sugar
4 chicken breast fillets
2 mangoes, thinly sliced
4 spring onions, sliced
1/4 cup (7 g/1/4 oz) coriander
   leaves
1/3 cup (45 g/1 1/2 oz) coarsely
   chopped roasted unsalted
   macadamia nuts

Dressing
2 tablespoons oil
1 teaspoon finely grated lime
   rind
2 tablespoons lime juice

1 Place the coconut milk, nam pla and palm sugar in a frying pan and bring to the boil, stirring. Reduce the heat, add the chicken fillets and gently simmer, covered, for 10 minutes, or until the chicken is just tender. Leave to cool in the coconut liquid, then remove and pour the liquid into a jug.
2 To make the dressing, put 1/2 cup (125 ml/4 fl oz) of the reserved coconut cooking liquid, the oil, lime rind and juice in a small bowl and whisk to combine. Season to taste with salt and pepper.
3 Cut each chicken fillet diagonally into long slices and arrange on individual serving plates or in a large serving bowl. Spoon the dressing over the chicken and top with the sliced mango, spring onion, coriander leaves and macadamia nuts.

NUTRITION PER SERVE
Protein 30 g; Fat 35 g; Carbohydrate 15 g;
Dietary Fibre 2 g; Cholesterol 55 mg;
1965 kJ (465 cal)

COOK'S FILE

Note: Palm sugar is obtained from either the palmyra palm or sugar palm, and is available in block form or in jars. It can be grated or gently melted before using. Soft brown sugar may be substituted.

Cut the mangoes into thin slices and remove the skin.

Using a sharp knife, coarsely chop the macadamia nuts.

Put the coconut milk, nam pla and palm sugar in a pan.

Cut each cooked chicken fillet into long diagonal slices.

BEEF, GREEN BEAN AND CHERRY TOMATO SALAD

Preparation time: 30 minutes
+ 2 hours marinating
Total cooking time: 10 minutes
Serves 4–6

500 g (1 lb) piece rump steak
1/2 teaspoon cracked black
    pepper
2 cloves garlic, crushed
2 teaspoons sesame oil
1 tablespoon honey
2 tablespoons soy sauce
2 tablespoons olive oil
500 g (1 lb) green beans
1 tablespoon sesame seeds
250 g (8 oz) cherry tomatoes,
    halved

Dressing
2 cloves garlic, crushed
1 teaspoon honey
2 tablespoons olive oil
2 tablespoons white wine
    vinegar
2 tablespoons soy sauce
2 teaspoons sesame oil

1 Trim the steak of any excess fat. Place the pepper, garlic, sesame oil, honey, soy sauce and olive oil in a large bowl and whisk to combine. Add the steak and toss to coat. Cover and refrigerate for 2 hours. Turn the steak in the marinade after 1 hour.
2 Meanwhile, top and tail the beans and add to a large pan of boiling water. Cook for 2 minutes, then plunge into a bowl of iced water to cool. Drain and set aside. Heat a small frying pan, add the sesame seeds and toss gently over low heat until they begin to brown.

3 To make the dressing, put all the ingredients in a screw-top jar and shake well to combine.
4 Chargrill the steak for 4–6 minutes, or until just cooked, depending on the thickness of the steak. Cool slightly, then slice thinly. Pile the beans on individual plates or on a serving

platter and scatter with the tomatoes. Lay the beef slices on top, drizzle with the dressing and sprinkle with the sesame seeds.

NUTRITION PER SERVE (6)
Protein 25 g; Fat 20 g; Carbohydrate 8 g; Dietary Fibre 3 g; Cholesterol 55 mg; 1255 kJ (300 cal)

Using a sharp knife, trim the steak of any excess fat.

Top and tail the green beans using a sharp vegetable knife.

Chargrill the marinated steak until it is just cooked.

TANDOORI CHICKEN SALAD

Preparation time: 20 minutes
+ overnight standing
Total cooking time: 15 minutes
Serves 4

4 chicken breast fillets
2–3 tablespoons tandoori paste
200 g (6¹/2 oz) plain thick
    yoghurt
1 tablespoon lemon juice
¹/2 cup (15 g/¹/2 oz) coriander
    leaves
¹/2 cup (60 g/2 oz) slivered
    almonds, toasted
snow pea sprouts, to serve

Cucumber and Yoghurt Dressing
1 Lebanese cucumber, grated
200 g (6¹/2 oz) plain thick
    yoghurt
1 tablespoon chopped mint
2 teaspoons lemon juice

1 Cut the chicken breast fillets into thick strips. Combine the tandoori paste, yoghurt and lemon juice in a large bowl, add the chicken strips and toss to coat well. Refrigerate and leave to marinate overnight.

2 To make the dressing, put the grated cucumber in a medium bowl. Add the yoghurt, chopped mint and lemon juice, and stir until well combined. Refrigerate until needed.

3 Heat a large non-stick frying pan, add the marinated chicken in batches and cook, turning frequently, until cooked through. Cool and place in a large bowl. Add the coriander leaves and toasted almonds, and toss until well combined. Serve on a bed of

snow pea sprouts, with the dressing served separately.

NUTRITION PER SERVE
Protein 35 g; Fat 15 g; Carbohydrate 7 g; Dietary Fibre 2 g; Cholesterol 70 mg; 1230 kJ (290 cal)

COOK'S FILE

Note: The quality of the tandoori paste used will determine the flavour and look of the chicken. There are many home-made varieties available from supermarkets and delicatessens.

Combine the tandoori paste, yoghurt and lemon juice.

Using a metal grater, coarsely grate the Lebanese cucumber.

Cook the marinated chicken in batches, turning frequently.

PROSCIUTTO, MIXED CRESS AND EGG SALAD

Preparation time: 20 minutes
Total cooking time: 10 minutes
Serves 4

3 eggs
250 g (8 oz) watercress
1 baby fennel bulb, thinly sliced
1 leek, thinly sliced
25 g (3/4 oz) mustard cress
80 g (2¾ oz) thinly sliced prosciutto, trimmed and cut into wide strips

Dressing
⅓ cup (80 ml/2¾ fl oz) extra virgin olive oil
½ teaspoon finely grated orange rind
2 tablespoons orange juice
3 teaspoons wholegrain mustard

1 Cook the eggs in a pan of simmering water for 8 minutes. Drain and cool briefly under cold running water and then leave in a bowl of cold water for 15 minutes. Shell and cut into quarters.
2 Trim the coarse stems from the watercress and combine with the fennel and leek slices on a serving plate or in a shallow bowl. Toss two thirds of the mustard cress with the prosciutto and arrange over the greens. Top with the egg quarters, then sprinkle with the remaining mustard cress.
3 To make the dressing, mix all the ingredients together well, then season to taste with salt and freshly ground black pepper. Drizzle over the salad and serve.

NUTRITION PER SERVE
Protein 10 g; Fat 25 g; Carbohydrate 5 g; Dietary Fibre 6 g; Cholesterol 145 mg; 1190 kJ (285 cal)

Thinly slice the baby fennel bulb, discarding the green tops.

Trim and discard the coarse stems from the watercress.

Season the dressing with freshly ground black pepper.

Sandwich Fillings

EGG AND MIXED CRESS SALAD

Combine 1/2 cup (125 g/4 oz) mayonnaise with 1 tablespoon chopped capers and 1 tablespoon wholegrain mustard. Spread half this mixture onto twelve slices of dark rye bread. Top six of the bread slices with 2 cups (60 g/2 oz) watercress, 6 thinly sliced hard-boiled eggs, 1 cup (45 g/1 1/2 oz) mustard cress or alfalfa sprouts, salt and freshly ground black pepper. Drizzle with the remaining mayonnaise mixture. Top with the other six slices. Serves 6

NUTRITION PER SERVE: Protein 15 g; Fat 15 g; Carbohydrate 40 g; Dietary Fibre 8 g; Cholesterol 215 mg; 1500 kJ (355 cal)

COLD MEAT AND MUSTARD SALAD

Steam or boil 2 small carrots until tender. Cut into small dice and combine with 2 chopped spring onions, 1 thinly sliced celery stick including the leaves, 1 chopped gherkin and 140 g (4 1/2 oz) chopped cooked ham, corned beef or other cold meat. Combine 1 tablespoon Dijon mustard, 2 teaspoons lemon juice, 2 tablespoons mayonnaise, 2 tablespoons sour cream and 2 teaspoons chopped dill and add to the salad. Mix until combined. Season with salt and pepper. Put two thinly sliced tomatoes on lavash bread, top with the salad and roll up. Serves 4

NUTRITION PER SERVE: Protein 15 g; Fat 10 g; Carbohydrate 40 g; Dietary Fibre 5 g; Cholesterol 35 mg; 1370 kJ (325 cal)

COTTAGE CHEESE, ASPARAGUS AND AVOCADO SALAD

Split open four bagels. Top with 2 cups (500 g/1 lb) cottage cheese combined with 1/2 cup (10 g/1/4 oz) chervil or parsley leaves. Blanch 155 g (5 oz) asparagus, drain well and cut into short lengths. Place 12 semi-dried tomatoes, 1 thinly sliced avocado and the asparagus on top of the cottage cheese, season with salt and freshly ground black pepper, and replace the tops. Serves 4

NUTRITION PER SERVE: Protein 30 g; Fat 30 g; Carbohydrate 40 g; Dietary Fibre 6 g; Cholesterol 45 mg; 2310 kJ (550 cal)

EGGPLANT AND ROCKET SALAD

Cut 400 g (12 3/4 oz) eggplant into quarters lengthways. Cut 1 red capsicum into quarters lengthways, removing the seeds and membrane. Bake the vegetables in a moderate 180°C (350°F/Gas 4) oven for 1 hour, or until soft and tender. Cool and cut into small pieces. Combine the vegetables with 100 g (3 1/4 oz) quartered cherry tomatoes, 2 chopped spring onions, 100 g (3 1/4 oz) crumbled feta cheese, 2 tablespoons each of coarsely chopped flat-leaf parsley and mint leaves, 1 tablespoon chopped capers, 1 finely chopped clove garlic, 1/4 cup (60 ml/2 fl oz) lemon juice and 2 tablespoons olive oil. Season with salt and freshly ground black pepper. Split 4 slices of Turkish bread open. Arrange 150 g (5 oz) rocket leaves on the bottom slices, top with the salad and replace the tops. Serves 4

NUTRITION PER SERVE: Protein 10 g; Fat 15 g; Carbohydrate 25 g; Dietary Fibre 6 g; Cholesterol 15 mg; 1180 kJ (280 cal)

TUNA SALAD

Drain a 425 g (13 1/2 oz) can of tuna in oil. Break up the tuna with a fork and combine with 2 chopped hard-boiled eggs, 3 chopped spring onions, 2 teaspoons grated lemon rind, 1 chopped celery stick, 1 tablespoon chopped flat-leaf parsley, 1/2 cup (125 g/4 oz) mayonnaise, 1/4 cup (60 g/2 oz) sour cream, salt and freshly ground black pepper to taste. Mix lightly with a fork. Serve with mixed lettuce leaves on bread rolls. Serves 4

NUTRITION PER SERVE: Protein 40 g; Fat 35 g; Carbohydrate 50 g; Dietary Fibre 7 g; Cholesterol 175 mg; 2900 kJ (690 cal)

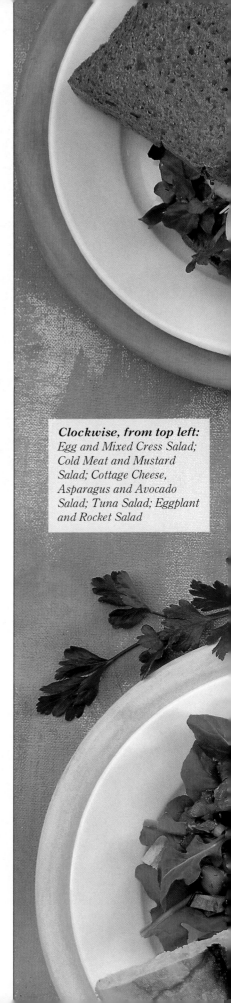

Clockwise, from top left: Egg and Mixed Cress Salad; Cold Meat and Mustard Salad; Cottage Cheese, Asparagus and Avocado Salad; Tuna Salad; Eggplant and Rocket Salad

DUCK AND RICE SALAD WITH SWEET GINGER DRESSING

Preparation time: 30 minutes
Total cooking time: 1 hour
Serves 4–6

Dressing
1/3 cup (80 ml/2³/4 fl oz) oil
1 teaspoon walnut oil
1 teaspoon grated orange rind
1 tablespoon orange juice
1 tablespoon finely chopped
  preserved ginger
1 teaspoon sambal oelek
1 teaspoon white wine vinegar

100 g (3¹/4 oz) wild rice
oil, for cooking
50 g (1³/4 oz) pecans
1/2 teaspoon ground cumin
1/2 teaspoon garam masala
1/4 teaspoon cayenne pepper
75 g (2¹/2 oz) long-grain white
  rice
1 celery stick, finely sliced
20 yellow pear tomatoes, cut in
  half lengthways
20 g (³/4 oz) French spinach or
  small English spinach leaves
4 spring onions, thinly sliced
450 g (14¹/4 oz) Chinese
  barbecued duck, with skin,
  cut into pieces
strips of orange rind, to garnish

1 To make the dressing, mix the ingredients together thoroughly. Season with salt and black pepper.
2 Rinse the wild rice under cold water and add to 300 ml (10 fl oz) of simmering water. Cook, covered, for 45 minutes, or until the grains puff open. Drain off any excess water.

3 Meanwhile, heat 2 teaspoons oil in a large frying pan. Add the pecans and cook, stirring, until golden. Remove from the pan and allow to cool. Coarsely chop the nuts. Add the cumin, garam masala, cayenne pepper and a pinch of salt to the pan, and cook for 1 minute, or until aromatic. Add the pecans and toss to coat.
4 Add the white rice to a pan of boiling water and simmer until tender. Drain and mix with the wild rice and pecans in a large, shallow bowl. Add the celery, tomato, spinach and spring

onion. Add half of the dressing and toss well. Arrange the pieces of duck on top with the skin uppermost. Drizzle with the remaining dressing and garnish with the orange rind.

NUTRITION PER SERVE (6)
Protein 20 g; Fat 40 g; Carbohydrate 30 g; Dietary Fibre 6 g; Cholesterol 90 mg; 2325 kJ (555 cal)

COOK'S FILE

Note: Chinese barbecued duck can be purchased from any Chinatown, or from your local Chinese restaurant.

Finely slice the celery stick, and halve the pear tomatoes lengthways.

Cook the wild rice, covered, until the grains puff open.

Return the chopped pecans to the pan and toss until well coated with the spices.

CARAMELISED BEEF, TOMATO AND ONION SALAD

Preparation time: 20 minutes
Total cooking time: 50 minutes
Serves 4

500 g (1 lb) beef fillet
2 tablespoons wholegrain
  mustard
1 tablespoon cracked black
  pepper
1/3 cup (80 ml/2³/4 fl oz) oil
1/4 cup (45 g/1¹/2 oz) soft brown
  sugar
6 baby onions, halved
200 g (6¹/2 oz) cherry tomatoes
250 g (8 oz) Camembert cheese
2 tablespoons chopped parsley

1 Preheat the oven to moderately hot 200°C (400°F/Gas 6). Tie the beef fillet neatly with kitchen string so it will hold its shape during cooking. Combine the mustard and pepper and rub over the fillet.

2 Heat half the oil in a frying pan and cook the fillet over high heat until browned. Transfer to a baking dish and bake for 20 minutes, or until medium rare. Remove from the oven and leave for 10 minutes.

3 Place the remaining oil and the brown sugar in a clean frying pan and cook, stirring, over low heat until the sugar dissolves. Add the onions and cook for 20 minutes, or until they are very soft and caramelised. Add the tomatoes and cook for 5 minutes, or until the skins soften. Be careful not to overcook the tomatoes or they will become mushy.

4 Thinly slice the beef fillet and Camembert. Arrange slices of beef on a serving plate and top with a slice of Camembert. Continue layering until all the beef and Camembert have been used. Pour any leftover pan juices from the beef into the pan with the onion and tomato.

5 Remove the onion and tomato from the pan and pile onto the centre of the salad. Drizzle with the pan juices and sprinkle with the parsley.

NUTRITION PER SERVE
Protein 40 g; Fat 40 g; Carbohydrate 20 g; Dietary Fibre 3 g; Cholesterol 140 mg; 2515 kJ (600 cal)

Tie the beef fillet neatly and firmly with kitchen string.

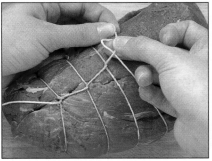

Stir the oil and brown sugar over low heat until the sugar dissolves.

Add the cherry tomatoes and cook until the skins soften.

Using a sharp knife, cut the Camembert cheese into thin slices.

MOROCCAN LAMB SALAD

Preparation time: 30 minutes
+ 1 hour marinating
Total cooking time: 10 minutes
Serves 4

500 g (1 lb) lamb backstrap
    (tender eye of the lamb loin)
1 teaspoon ground cumin
1/2 teaspoon turmeric
2 teaspoons harissa
2 tablespoons oil
3 oranges, segmented
1 red onion, sliced
1/4 preserved lemon, rind only,
    finely chopped
2 tablespoons shredded mint

1/4 cup (7 g/1/4 oz) coriander
    leaves
2 small red chillies, cut into
    very thin strips, to garnish

Dressing
2 cloves garlic, crushed
1/2 teaspoon ground cumin
1 tablespoon lemon juice
1/4 cup (60 ml/2 fl oz) olive oil

1 Trim any excess fat or sinew from
the lamb and place in a shallow dish.
Combine the cumin, turmeric, harissa
and oil, pour over the lamb and toss to
coat. Cover and refrigerate for 1 hour.
2 To make the dressing, whisk all the
ingredients together in a bowl.
3 Combine the orange, onion, lemon

rind and herbs. Drizzle with the
dressing, mix gently and refrigerate.
4 Cook the marinated lamb on a
preheated barbecue grill or in a
chargrill pan for 5 minutes on each
side, or until medium rare. Leave for
10 minutes before slicing. Divide the
salad among four plates, top with the
sliced lamb, garnish with the chilli
strips and serve.

NUTRITION PER SERVE
Protein 30 g; Fat 30 g; Carbohydrate 9 g;
Dietary Fibre 3 g; Cholesterol 80 mg;
1730 kJ (410 cal)

COOK'S FILE

Note: Harissa is made of spices, chilli
peppers, garlic and oil. It is available
from supermarkets and delicatessens.

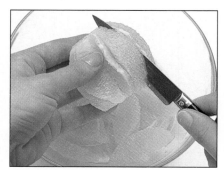

*Peel and segment the oranges using a
small sharp knife.*

*Combine the orange segments, red onion,
preserved lemon rind and herbs.*

*Cook the marinated lamb for 5 minutes
on each side.*

WARM QUAIL SALAD

Preparation time: 20 minutes
+ 2 hours marinating
Total cooking time: 10 minutes
Serves 4

8 quails
1/2 cup (125 ml/4 fl oz) oil
1/2 cup (125 ml/4 fl oz) soy
  sauce
2 tablespoons honey
2 tablespoons dry sherry
1 tablespoon grated fresh ginger
105 g (3 1/2 oz) rocket leaves

Dressing
1/3 cup (80 ml/2 3/4 fl oz) olive oil
rind of 1 orange, shredded and
  blanched (see Note)
1/4 cup (60 ml/2 fl oz) fresh
  orange juice
1 tablespoon balsamic vinegar

1 Cut the quail in half down either side of the backbone and down the centre of the breast bone. Discard the backbone. Rinse well under cold water and pat dry with paper towels. Place the oil, soy sauce, honey, sherry and ginger in a shallow dish and whisk to combine. Add the quail and toss to coat well. Cover and marinate for 2 hours, turning occasionally, or cover and refrigerate overnight, if desired.
2 Preheat the grill to moderately hot. Drain the quail and place on a shallow baking tray, reserving the marinade. Grill for about 8–10 minutes, or until cooked, turning once. Baste with the marinade during cooking.
3 To make the dressing, put the ingredients in a small bowl and whisk to combine. Season to taste with salt and pepper.
4 Arrange the rocket leaves on individual serving plates with the quail. Drizzle with the dressing and serve immediately.

NUTRITION PER SERVE
Protein 75 g; Fat 65 g; Carbohydrate 15 g; Dietary Fibre 1 g; Cholesterol 250 mg; 3940 kJ (940 cal)

COOK'S FILE

Note: To blanch the orange rind, bring a small pan of water to the boil. Add the orange rind and simmer for 1 minute, then drain.

Using poultry shears, cut the quail in half down the backbone and breast bone.

Place the marinated quail on a baking tray and grill until cooked.

Baste the quail occasionally with the marinade during cooking.

Remove all the white pith from the orange rind, and shred it finely.

SMOKED TOFU SALAD WITH SPICY COCONUT DRESSING

Preparation time: 15 minutes
Total cooking time: Nil
Serves 4–6

Spicy Coconut Dressing
50 ml (1³/4 fl oz) coconut cream
1 tablespoon peanut oil
1/2 teaspoon sesame oil
1/2 teaspoon fish sauce
2 teaspoons lemon juice
2 teaspoons sweet chilli sauce, or to taste

100 g (3¹/4 oz) red cabbage, shredded
100 g (3¹/4 oz) Chinese cabbage, shredded
350 g (11¹/4 oz) Chinese barbecued pork, sliced
50 g (1³/4 oz) leek, thinly sliced
100 g (3¹/4 oz) smoked tofu, cut into 1 cm (1/2 inch) cubes
Vietnamese mint leaves and opal basil leaves, to garnish

1 To make the dressing, whisk the ingredients together. Season with salt and freshly ground black pepper.
2 Combine the cabbage, pork, leek and tofu in a large bowl. Pour in the dressing and toss through. Sprinkle with the mint and basil leaves.

NUTRITION PER SERVE (6)
Protein 15 g; Fat 15 g; Carbohydrate 4 g; Dietary Fibre 3 g; Cholesterol 35 mg; 865 kJ (205 cal)

COOK'S FILE

Note: Chinese barbecued pork can be purchased from barbecue counters in any Chinatown or from some Asian food stores. It can also be bought from Chinese take-away outlets and will be sold pre-sliced. Smoked tofu is available from supermarkets and Asian food stores. If smoked is unavailable, use baked tofu.

Finely shred the red cabbage and the Chinese cabbage.

Mix together the coconut cream, oils, fish sauce, lemon juice and sweet chilli sauce.

Combine the cabbage, pork, leek and tofu in a large bowl.

MEDITERRANEAN SALAD

Preparation time: 25 minutes
Total cooking time: 5 minutes
Serves 4–6

oil, for cooking
4 chorizo sausages, thickly
    sliced
150 g (5 oz) rocket
2 red capsicums, cut into pieces
2 green capsicums, cut into
    pieces
1 fennel bulb, thinly sliced
4 egg (Roma) tomatoes, cut into
    wedges

2 Lebanese cucumbers,
    sliced
300 g (10 oz) marinated
    artichokes, quartered
2 tablespoons chopped dill
250 g (8 oz) feta cheese, broken
    into large pieces

Dressing
1 teaspoon finely grated orange
    rind
1/4 cup (60 ml/2 fl oz) orange
    juice
2 teaspoons red wine vinegar
1 clove garlic, crushed
1/4 cup (60 ml/2 fl oz) olive
    oil

1 Heat a little oil in a non-stick frying pan. Fry the chorizo slices in batches until browned. Drain on paper towels.
2 Trim the coarse stems from the rocket and combine with the fried chorizo slices, capsicum, fennel, tomato, cucumber, artichokes, dill and feta in a bowl.
3 To make the dressing, put the orange rind and juice, vinegar, garlic and oil in a bowl, and whisk to combine. Pour over the salad and toss gently to coat.

NUTRITION PER SERVE (6)
Protein 15 g; Fat 35 g; Carbohydrate 10 g;
Dietary Fibre 7 g; Cholesterol 50 mg;
1700 kJ (405 cal)

Thickly slice the chorizo sausages, and cut the capsicums into large pieces.

Use your fingers to break the feta cheese into large pieces.

Fry the chorizo in a little oil, then drain on paper towels.

CHILLI SALT CHICKEN SALAD

Preparation time: 35 minutes
Total cooking time: 20 minutes
Serves 4

1 red capsicum, cut into julienne strips (see Note)
1 yellow capsicum, cut into julienne strips
4 spring onions, cut into julienne strips
1 cup (20 g/3/4 oz) mint leaves
1 cup (30 g/1 oz) coriander leaves
3 chicken breast fillets
1/2 cup (60 g/2 oz) plain flour
1 tablespoon chilli powder
1 tablespoon onion powder
1 tablespoon garlic powder
1 tablespoon finely crushed sea salt
oil, for deep-frying

Dressing
1 tablespoon sugar
2 tablespoons lemon juice
1/4 cup (60 ml/2 fl oz) rice vinegar
1/4 cup (60 ml/2 fl oz) peanut oil

1 Put the capsicum and spring onion strips in a bowl with the mint and coriander leaves.
2 To make the dressing, put the sugar, lemon juice, vinegar and oil in a bowl and whisk to combine.
3 Cut the chicken fillets into thin strips. Combine the flour, chilli powder, onion powder, garlic powder and salt in a plastic bag or shallow bowl. Add the chicken in batches and toss to coat in the flour mix. Remove and shake off any excess flour.

4 Half fill a large heavy-based pan with the oil. When the oil is hot, add the chicken in batches and deep-fry until it is golden brown. Drain well on paper towels. Add the chicken to the bowl with the vegetables and herbs, drizzle with the dressing and toss gently to combine. Serve immediately.

NUTRITION PER SERVE
Protein 20 g; Fat 30 g; Carbohydrate 20 g; Dietary Fibre 2 g; Cholesterol 40 mg; 1720 kJ (410 cal)

COOK'S FILE

Note: Julienne strips are even-sized strips of vegetables, the size and shape of matchsticks.

Cut the capsicums and spring onions into julienne strips.

Cut the chicken breast fillets into long, thin strips.

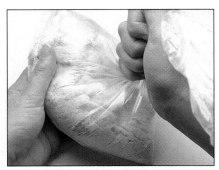
Add the chicken to the spiced flour and toss to coat.

ROAST TOMATO, EGG AND SALAMI SALAD

Preparation time: 15 minutes
Total cooking time: 30 minutes
Serves 6

12 egg (Roma) tomatoes, halved lengthways
1 bulb garlic, cloves separated
1 teaspoon fine sea salt flakes
8 eggs, hard-boiled and quartered

100 g (3¼ oz) marinated black olives
50 g (1¾ oz) spicy salami, sliced into thin strips
3 spring onions, sliced
2 tablespoons shredded basil leaves
2 tablespoons extra virgin olive oil
2 tablespoons balsamic vinegar

1 Preheat the oven to moderately hot 200°C (400°F/Gas 6). Put the tomato halves and garlic on a baking tray, sprinkle with the sea salt and some cracked black pepper and bake for 30 minutes, or until tender.

2 Arrange the tomato halves on a serving platter, top with the garlic, hard-boiled eggs, olives, salami, spring onion and basil.

3 Drizzle the olive oil and balsamic vinegar over the salad. Serve the salad hot or cold.

NUTRITION PER SERVE
Protein 10 g; Fat 20 g; Carbohydrate 4 g; Dietary Fibre 3 g; Cholesterol 285 mg; 1005 kJ (240 cal)

Pull the bulb of garlic apart to separate the individual cloves.

Slice the spring onions, and shred the basil leaves.

Sprinkle the tomato halves and garlic cloves with the sea salt flakes.

SEAFOOD

MIXED SEAFOOD SALAD

Preparation time: 1 hour
 + 1 hour refrigeration
Total cooking time: 20 minutes
Serves 8

20 cooked king prawns
12 cooked yabbies
1/2 cup (125 ml/4 fl oz) white
 wine
pinch of dried thyme
pinch of dried tarragon or a bay
 leaf
20 scallops, with roe attached
400 g (12³/4 oz) salmon, trout or
 firm white fish fillets
1 quantity of Basic Vinaigrette
 (see page 18)
2 teaspoons Dijon mustard
1 tablespoon chopped dill
6 hard-boiled eggs
150 g (5 oz) mesclun (mixed
 lettuce leaves)
2 tablespoons coarsely chopped
 flat-leaf parsley
2 avocados, sliced
2 tablespoons lemon juice
1 quantity of Green Goddess
 Dressing (see page 101)

1 Peel and devein the prawns. Using a sharp knife, cut lengthways through the centre of the yabbies. Lift out the flesh in one piece, remove the veins and discard the shells.
2 Put 1 cup (250 ml/8 fl oz) water with the wine, herbs and a pinch of salt and pepper in a pan. Bring to the boil, then reduce the heat and simmer for 5 minutes. Add the scallops and poach for a few minutes, or until they have just turned white, then remove with a slotted spoon and drain on a wire rack. Add the fish fillets to the simmering liquid. Poach until cooked and just tender, remove with a slotted spoon and drain on a wire rack. Break into large pieces.
3 Combine the prawns, yabbies, scallops and fish in a bowl. Whisk together the Vinaigrette, mustard and dill. Pour into the bowl, cover and refrigerate for 1 hour. Peel and slice the eggs, reserving 2 yolks.
4 Place half the lettuce leaves in the base of a deep serving bowl. Arrange about half the seafood on the lettuce, reserving the dill vinaigrette. Sprinkle with half the parsley, top with half the avocado, drizzle with half the lemon juice, then finish with half the sliced eggs, including the extra whites. Season with salt and pepper. Repeat the layers and season to taste. Drizzle with the reserved dill vinaigrette. Crumble the reserved egg yolks over the top and serve with the Green Goddess Dressing.

NUTRITION PER SERVE
Protein 50 g; Fat 70 g; Carbohydrate 3 g; Dietary Fibre 3 g; Cholesterol 435 mg; 3475 kJ (825 cal)

COOK'S FILE

Note: If yabbies are not available, use crayfish instead.

Cut the yabbies lengthways through the soft shell and lift out the flesh.

Using a pair of tongs, lower the scallops into the poaching liquid.

CHARGRILLED TUNA AND RUBY GRAPEFRUIT SALAD

Preparation time: 20 minutes
Total cooking time: 10 minutes
Serves 4–6

4 ruby grapefruit
oil, for cooking
3 tuna steaks
150 g (5 oz) rocket leaves
1 red onion, sliced

Almond and Raspberry Dressing
2 tablespoons almond oil
2 tablespoons raspberry vinegar
1/2 teaspoon sugar
1 tablespoon shredded mint

1 Cut a slice off each end of the grapefruit and peel away the skin, removing all the pith. Separate the segments and set aside in a bowl.
2 Heat a chargrill plate and brush lightly with oil. Cook each tuna steak for 3–4 minutes on each side. This will leave the centre slightly pink. Cool, then thinly slice or flake.
3 To make the dressing, put the almond oil, vinegar, sugar and mint in a small screw-top jar and shake until well combined.
4 Place the rocket on a serving plate and top with the grapefruit segments, then the tuna and onion. Drizzle with the dressing and serve.

NUTRITION PER SERVE (6)
Protein 15 g; Fat 15 g; Carbohydrate 8 g; Dietary Fibre 2 g; Cholesterol 50 mg; 1015 kJ (240 cal)

Cut a slice off the ends of the grapefruit and peel away the skin and pith.

Separate the grapefruit into segments and set aside in a bowl.

Cook the tuna steaks on a lightly oiled chargrill plate.

MELON AND CRAB SALAD WITH REDCURRANT MINT DRESSING

Preparation time: 1 hour
Total cooking time: 2 minutes
Serves 4

6 large cooked blue swimmer
    crabs, or 375 g (12 oz)
    frozen crab meat, thawed and
    squeezed dry
1/4 small honeydew melon
1/4 small watermelon
1/4 small rockmelon
1 mizuna lettuce, washed, dried
    and chilled
2 ruby grapefruit, segmented
nasturtium flowers, to garnish

Redcurrant Mint Dressing
2 tablespoons redcurrant jelly
2 tablespoons red wine vinegar
1/2 cup (125 ml/4 fl oz) light
    olive oil
1 tablespoon finely shredded
    mint

1 To prepare the whole crabs, use
your thumb to pull the apron back
and lift off the crab shell. Pull away
the white gills along the sides and
discard. Wash the crab well. Remove
the flesh from the body with your
fingers. Crack the legs open using a
nutcracker and remove the flesh.
2 Remove the seeds and skin from
the melons and chop the flesh or use a
melon baller to scoop out rounds.
3 To make the dressing, heat the jelly
and vinegar in a small pan over low
heat until the jelly has dissolved.
Allow to cool, then gradually whisk in
the olive oil until it has a smooth
consistency. Add the shredded mint
and season to taste with salt and
freshly ground black pepper.
4 Tear the mizuna into pieces and
arrange with the pieces of melon and
grapefruit segments on individual
serving plates. Top each with some of
the crab meat and drizzle with the
dressing. Serve garnished with the
nasturtium flowers.

NUTRITION PER SERVE
Protein 15 g; Fat 30 g; Carbohydrate 15 g;
Dietary Fibre 3 g; Cholesterol 80 mg;
1665 kJ (395 cal)

*Using your thumb, pull back the apron
and lift off the crab shell.*

*Pull away the white gills from the sides of
the crab.*

*Chop the melons or use a melon baller to
scoop out rounds.*

*Heat the redcurrant jelly and vinegar
until the jelly has dissolved.*

CHARGRILLED BABY OCTOPUS SALAD

Preparation time: 30 minutes
  + 2 hours marinating
Total cooking time: 10 minutes
Serves 4–6

1 kg (2 lb) baby octopus
2 limes
1/4 cup (60 ml/2 fl oz) sweet
  chilli sauce
1 tablespoon soy sauce
5 cm (2 inch) piece ginger,
  grated

2 cloves garlic, crushed
2 spring onions, sliced
mixed lettuce leaves, to serve
lime wedges, to serve

1 Using a sharp knife, remove and discard the head from the octopus. (The head can be cleaned and added if desired.) Pick up the body and, using your index finger, push the beak up to remove and discard.
2 Using a vegetable peeler, peel the rind from the limes, avoiding the white pith. Cut the rind into thin strips. Squeeze the limes to get 2 tablespoons of juice.

3 Combine the chilli sauce, soy sauce, ginger, garlic, lime zest and juice. Add the octopus and toss to coat. Cover and refrigerate for 2 hours.
4 Heat a chargrill plate and lightly brush with oil. Cook the octopus in batches for 3–5 minutes, or until the flesh turns white and tender. Place the cooked octopus in a bowl, add the spring onion and serve on a bed of mixed lettuce leaves, accompanied by the lime wedges.

NUTRITION PER SERVE (6)
Protein 25 g; Fat 2 g; Carbohydrate 5 g;
Dietary Fibre 1 g; Cholesterol 0 mg;
580 kJ (140 cal)

Push the beak of the octopus up with your index finger.

Combine the chilli sauce, soy sauce, ginger, garlic, lime zest and lime juice.

Cook the octopus on a lightly oiled chargrill plate.

SALMON AND GREEN BEAN SALAD

Preparation time: 20 minutes
Total cooking time: 30 minutes
Serves 4–6

350 g (11¼ oz) salmon fillet
oil, for deep-frying
4 cloves garlic, thinly sliced
200 g (6½ oz) white sweet
    potato, thinly sliced
100 g (3¼ oz) green beans,
    halved lengthways
1 red onion, thinly sliced

20 g (¾ oz) sesame seeds,
    toasted
1 mizuna lettuce, stems trimmed

Dressing
2 cloves garlic, crushed
2 tablespoons tahini
1 tablespoon rice vinegar
2 tablespoons lime juice
1 tablespoon soy sauce
¼ cup (60 ml/2 fl oz) olive oil

1 Chargrill or grill the salmon fillet until medium rare or cooked as desired. Cool slightly before cutting into large pieces.

2 Heat the oil and deep-fry the garlic and sweet potato separately until crisp and golden. Drain on paper towels.
3 Cook the beans in boiling water until tender. Rinse, plunge into iced water and drain. Combine with the onion, sesame seeds, sweet potato, garlic and mizuna. Divide among serving plates. Top with the salmon.
4 To make the dressing, whisk the ingredients in a bowl. Drizzle over the salad and serve immediately.

NUTRITION PER SERVE (6)
Protein 15 g; Fat 30 g; Carbohydrate 9 g; Dietary Fibre 4 g; Cholesterol 40 mg; 1605 kJ (380 cal)

Using a small sharp knife, halve the green beans lengthways.

Chargrill the whole salmon fillet until it is medium rare.

Deep-fry the sweet potato until it is crisp and golden.

SEAFOOD AND AVOCADO SALAD

Preparation time: 30 minutes
Total cooking time: 35 minutes
Serves 4

350 g (11¼ oz) orange sweet
    potato, cubed
1 tablespoon virgin olive oil
40 g (1¼ oz) butter
1 teaspoon oil
1 clove garlic
250 g (8 oz) scallops, trimmed
2 teaspoons lemon juice
24 raw prawns (about 600 g/
    1¼ lb), peeled and deveined,
    tails intact
½ mizuna lettuce
½ red oakleaf lettuce
1 Lebanese cucumber, peeled,
    seeded and cut into thin
    slices
2 avocados, thickly sliced
1 tablespoon chopped opal or
    green basil
opal or green basil leaves, to
    garnish

Dressing
120 g (4 oz) butter
2 egg yolks
1 tablespoon white wine vinegar
2 tablespoons lime juice

1 Preheat the oven to moderately hot
190°C (375°F/Gas 5). Put the sweet
potato cubes in a shallow ovenproof
dish and toss to coat with the olive oil.
Spread in a single layer, so that the
cubes are not touching, then bake for
15 minutes. Sprinkle lightly with salt,
turn over, then bake for a further
10 minutes, or until just cooked. Leave
to cool.

2 Meanwhile, heat half the butter and
the oil in a large pan. Add the garlic
and stir for 10–15 seconds. Add the
scallops and sauté over medium-high
heat for 3–4 minutes, or until cooked
through but not browned. Sprinkle
with half the lemon juice and season
lightly with salt and white pepper.
Drain on paper towels.

3 Add the remaining butter to the
same pan and, when it foams, add the
prawns. Sauté over high heat for
2–3 minutes, or until crisp and
opaque. Sprinkle with the remaining
lemon juice and season lightly with
salt. Discard the garlic clove and drain
the prawns on paper towels.

4 Put the mizuna and oakleaf lettuce
leaves in a large, shallow bowl. Add

the cucumber, sweet potato, scallops
and prawns, and toss lightly. Arrange
the avocado slices over the top.

5 To make the dressing, melt the
butter and keep it hot. Blend the egg
yolks and vinegar in a food processor
for 5 seconds. With the machine still
running, slowly pour in the hot melted
butter (the heat will thicken the
mixture). Add the lime juice and
season with salt and white pepper.
Process briefly to combine. Drizzle
over the salad and toss lightly.
Sprinkle with the chopped basil and
garnish with the basil leaves.

NUTRITION PER SERVE
Protein 45 g; Fat 70 g; Carbohydrate 15 g;
Dietary Fibre 5 g; Cholesterol 435 mg;
3605 kJ (860 cal)

*Trim the dark vein from the scallops,
leaving the roe attached.*

*Add the prawns to the foaming butter
and sauté over high heat.*

*Blend the egg yolks and vinegar, and
slowly pour in the hot melted butter.*

PRAWN AND PAPAYA SALAD

Preparation time: 25 minutes
Total cooking time: 5 minutes
Serves 4

750 g (1½ lb) large raw prawns
1 large papaya, chopped
1 small red onion, finely sliced
2 celery sticks, finely sliced
2 tablespoons shredded mint
  leaves

Dressing
½ cup (125 ml/4 fl oz) oil
¼ cup (60 ml/2 fl oz) lime juice
2 teaspoons finely grated fresh
  ginger
1 teaspoon caster sugar

1 Peel and devein the prawns, leaving the tails intact. Place in a pan of boiling water, return to the boil, then simmer for 2–3 minutes, or until the prawns turn pink. Drain and place in a large bowl.
2 To make the dressing, put the lime juice, ginger and sugar in a small bowl and whisk to combine. Season to taste with salt and black pepper.
3 Add the dressing to the prawns, toss gently to coat and leave to cool. Add the papaya, onion, celery and mint and toss to combine. Serve the salad at room temperature, or cover and refrigerate for up to 3 hours before serving.

NUTRITION PER SERVE
Protein 40 g; Fat 31 g; Carbohydrate 10 g; Dietary Fibre 3 g; Cholesterol 280 mg; 1090 kJ (260 cal)

Finely slice the red onion and finely slice the celery sticks diagonally.

Make a slit along the back of the peeled prawns and remove the vein.

Whisk the dressing ingredients in a small bowl until combined.

83

CRAB AND MANGO SALAD

Preparation time: 25 minutes
Total cooking time: 5 minutes
Serves 4

Dressing
1/3 cup (80 ml/2¾ fl oz) light olive oil
1/4 cup (60 ml/2 fl oz) lime juice
1 teaspoon fish sauce
1/2 small green chilli, finely chopped
1 tablespoon finely chopped coriander
2 teaspoons grated fresh ginger

2 x 4 cm (1½ inch) square pieces of fresh coconut
1 teaspoon olive oil
2 cups (60 g/2 oz) trimmed watercress
100 g (3¼ oz) snow pea sprouts
400 g (12¾ oz) flaked crab meat (fresh, frozen or canned)
100 g (3¼ oz) cooked, peeled, small prawns
1 ripe but firm mango, peeled and cut into thin strips
coriander leaves and lime slices, to garnish

1 To make the dressing, combine the ingredients and season with salt and freshly ground black pepper. Set aside to allow the flavours to develop.
2 Peel the coconut into wafer-thin slices using a vegetable peeler. Heat the olive oil in a pan and gently fry the coconut, stirring, until golden. Drain on paper towels.
3 Combine the watercress and snow pea sprouts and arrange on a platter.

4 Lightly toss the crab meat, prawns, mango and three quarters of the toasted coconut together, then pour in the dressing. Pile in the centre of the watercress and snow pea sprout mixture, scatter the remaining coconut over the top and garnish with the coriander leaves and lime slices.

NUTRITION PER SERVE
Protein 20 g; Fat 25 g; Carbohydrate 7 g; Dietary Fibre 2 g; Cholesterol 130 mg; 1310 kJ (310 cal)

COOK'S FILE

Note: The coconut may be toasted in advance. If it becomes soft, toss in a lightly oiled pan until crisp.

Using a sharp knife, peel the mango and cut it into thin strips.

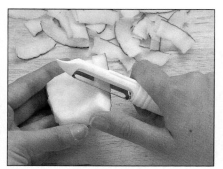

Peel the coconut into thin slices using a vegetable peeler.

Pour the dressing over the combined crab meat, prawns, mango and coconut.

WARM PRAWN, ROCKET AND FETA SALAD

Preparation time: 30 minutes
Total cooking time: 10 minutes
Serves 4–6

1 kg (2 lb) raw prawns
4 spring onions, chopped
4 egg (Roma) tomatoes, chopped
1 red capsicum, chopped
425 g (13½ oz) can chickpeas,
    drained
1 tablespoon chopped dill
¼ cup (15 g/½ oz) finely
    shredded basil
¼ cup (60 ml/2 fl oz) extra
    virgin olive oil
50 g (1¾ oz) butter
2 small red chillies, finely
    chopped
4 cloves garlic, crushed
2 tablespoons lemon juice
300 g (10 oz) rocket leaves
150 g (5 oz) feta cheese

1 Peel and devein the prawns, leaving the tails intact. Combine the spring onion, tomato, capsicum, chickpeas and herbs in a bowl.
2 Heat the oil and butter in a large frying pan or wok, add the prawns and cook over high heat for 3 minutes. Add the chilli and garlic, and continue cooking until the prawns turn pink. Remove from the heat and stir in the lemon juice.
3 Arrange the rocket leaves on a large platter, top with the tomato mixture, then the prawn mixture. Crumble the feta cheese over the top.

NUTRITION PER SERVE (6)
Protein 45 g; Fat 25 g; Carbohydrate 15 g;
Dietary Fibre 6 g; Cholesterol 285 mg;
1920 kJ (455 cal)

Chop the spring onions, tomatoes and red capsicum.

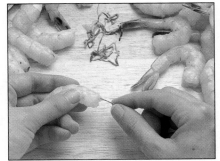

Gently pull the vein from the top of the prawns, without slitting the back.

Add the chilli and garlic to the prawns and cook until the prawns turn pink.

SMOKED TROUT SALAD WITH WARM CHILLI AND RASPBERRY DRESSING

Preparation time: 25 minutes
Total cooking time: 10 minutes
Serves 4–6

250 g (8 oz) sorrel
310 g (10 oz) fresh asparagus
1 whole smoked trout (about
　　400 g/12³/4 oz)
1 red onion, thinly sliced
250 g (8 oz) pear tomatoes,
　　halved
200 g (6¹/2 oz) fresh raspberries

Warm Chilli and Raspberry
*　Dressing*
125 g (4 oz) fresh raspberries
1 teaspoon chilli paste
2 cloves garlic, crushed
¹/2 cup (125 ml/4 fl oz) olive oil
2 tablespoons raspberry vinegar
　　(see Note)

1 Trim the stalks from the sorrel leaves, wash thoroughly in cold water, then dry and refrigerate to crisp.
2 To make the dressing, put the ingredients in a small pan and stir gently over low heat until the raspberries begin to break up and colour the liquid. Transfer to a bowl, whisk together well and season with salt and freshly ground black pepper.
3 Boil, steam or microwave the asparagus until just tender. Drain and rinse under cold water. Peel away the skin and remove the bones from the trout. Break the flesh into pieces.
4 Divide the sorrel among individual plates. Arrange the asparagus, trout, onion, tomatoes and raspberries on top. Drizzle with the dressing.

NUTRITION PER SERVE (6)
Protein 20 g; Fat 25 g; Carbohydrate 6 g; Dietary Fibre 7 g; Cholesterol 50 mg; 1355 kJ (320 cal)

COOK'S FILE

Note: If raspberry vinegar is not available, use white wine vinegar in this recipe.

Trim the stalks from the fresh sorrel leaves by snapping them off.

Stir the dressing over low heat until the raspberries begin to break up.

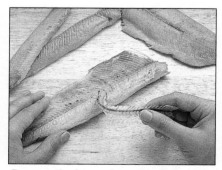

Remove the bones from the flesh of the smoked trout.

VEGETABLE AND SCALLOP SALAD

Preparation time: 40 minutes
Total cooking time: 15 minutes
Serves 4–6

1/4 red cabbage
1 carrot
2 celery sticks
1 red capsicum
1 green capsicum
1 yellow capsicum
100 g (3¼ oz) snow peas
300 g (10 oz) scallops
1 tablespoon black sesame seeds

Dressing
grated rind of 1 lime
90 ml (3 fl oz) lime juice
2 tablespoons fish sauce
1 tablespoon grated palm sugar
1 small red chilli, finely
   chopped
1/2 teaspoon sesame oil

1 Finely shred the red cabbage. Cut the carrot, celery, capsicums and snow peas into julienne strips, the size and shape of matchsticks.
2 Chargrill the scallops in batches on a lightly oiled barbecue grill pan until they are tender.
3 To make the dressing, put the lime rind and juice, fish sauce, sugar, chilli and oil in a small bowl. Whisk gently to combine.
4 Combine the chopped vegetables, chargrilled scallops and sesame seeds in a large bowl. Pour in the dressing and toss to coat.

NUTRITION PER SERVE (6)
Protein 10 g; Fat 2 g; Carbohydrate 8 g; Dietary Fibre 6 g; Cholesterol 15 mg; 405 kJ (95 cal)

COOK'S FILE

Note: Black sesame seeds are available from Asian food stores. If they are not available, they may be substituted with white sesame seeds.

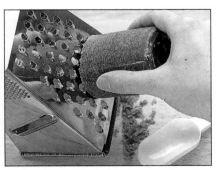

Using the coarse side of a metal grater, grate the palm sugar.

Cut the carrot, celery and capsicums into julienne strips.

Chargrill the scallops in batches until they are tender.

LIME AND PRAWN SALAD

Preparation time: 35 minutes
Total cooking time: 2 minutes
Serves 4

200 g (6¹/2 oz) baby green beans
2 Lebanese cucumbers, sliced
4 spring onions, finely chopped
1 tablespoon finely shredded
    kaffir lime leaves
¹/4 cup (15 g/¹/2 oz) flaked
    coconut
750 g (1¹/2 lb) cooked prawns,
    peeled, tails intact
2 teaspoons shredded lime rind

Dressing
1 tablespoon peanut oil
1 tablespoon nam pla (Thai fish
    sauce)
1 tablespoon grated palm sugar
1 tablespoon chopped coriander
2 teaspoons soy sauce
1–2 teaspoons sweet chilli sauce
¹/4 cup (60 ml/2 fl oz) lime juice

1 Cook the beans in a small pan of
boiling water for 2 minutes. Drain and
cover with cold water, then drain
again and pat dry with paper towels.
2 To make the dressing, whisk the
ingredients in a bowl to combine.
3 Combine the beans, cucumber,

spring onion, lime leaves, flaked
coconut and prawns in a large bowl.
Add the dressing and toss gently to
combine. Place the salad in a large
serving bowl and garnish with the
shredded lime rind.

NUTRITION PER SERVE
Protein 45 g; Fat 8 g; Carbohydrate 7 g;
Dietary Fibre 3 g; Cholesterol 350 mg;
1200 kJ (285 cal)

COOK'S FILE

Note: Young lemon leaves can be
used in place of the kaffir lime leaves
if they are not available.
Soft brown or dark brown sugar may
be substituted for the palm sugar.

*Cut the cucumbers in half lengthways,
then cut into slices.*

*Lower the beans into a small pan of
boiling water and cook for 2 minutes.*

*Whisk the dressing ingredients in a small
bowl until combined.*

WARM MUSSEL AND POTATO SALAD

Preparation time: 20 minutes
Total cooking time: 20 minutes
Serves 4

500 g (1 lb) baby new potatoes
1 kg (2 lb) fresh black mussels
45 g (1½ oz) baby English
  spinach leaves

Dressing
⅓ cup (80 ml/2¾ fl oz) olive oil
⅓ cup (80 ml/2¾ fl oz) cream
1 teaspoon grated lemon rind
2 tablespoons lemon juice
1 teaspoon caster sugar
1 tablespoon chopped lemon
  thyme

1 Cook the potatoes in boiling water until tender. Drain and keep warm.
2 Scrub the mussels well and remove the beards, discarding any that are open. Place in a pan with 2 cups (500 ml/16 fl oz) water, cover and cook gently until they have just opened. Do not overcook. Cover immediately with cold water and remove from the shells. Discard any mussels that have not opened. Pat dry with paper towels.
3 To make the dressing, put the oil, cream, lemon rind and juice, sugar and lemon thyme in a small bowl and whisk to combine. Season to taste with salt and pepper.
4 Combine the warm potatoes, mussels and spinach leaves in a large bowl. Add the dressing and toss gently. Serve immediately.

NUTRITION PER SERVE
Protein 45 g; Fat 35 g; Carbohydrate 20 g;
Dietary Fibre 2 g; Cholesterol 275 mg;
2310 kJ (550 cal)

Grate a lemon on the fine side of a grater to get 1 teaspoon of grated rind.

Cook the potatoes in boiling water until just tender.

Wash and scrub the mussels and remove the beards. Disard any that are open.

PASTA, RICE & PULSES

MEXICANA SALAD

Preparation time: 40 minutes
  + overnight standing
Total cooking time: 1 hour
Serves 10–12

250 g (8 oz) black-eyed beans
250 g (8 oz) red kidney beans
500 g (1 lb) sweet potato
1 large red onion, chopped
1 large green capsicum, chopped
3 ripe tomatoes, chopped
1/4 cup (15 g/1/2 oz) chopped
   basil
3 flour tortillas
1 tablespoon oil
2 tablespoons grated Parmesan
1/4 cup (60 g/2 oz) sour cream

Dressing
1 clove garlic, crushed
1 tablespoon lime juice
2 tablespoons olive oil

Guacamole
3 avocados
2 tablespoons lemon juice
1 clove garlic, crushed
1 small red onion, chopped
1 small red chilli, chopped
1/4 cup (60 g/2 oz) sour cream
2 tablespoons hot taco sauce

1 Soak the beans in a large bowl of cold water overnight. Drain and cook in a large pan of rapidly boiling water for 30 minutes, or until just tender. Skim off any scum that appears on the surface during cooking. Do not overcook or they will become mushy. Drain and set aside to cool.
2 Chop the sweet potato into large pieces and cook in boiling water until tender. Drain and combine with the onion, capsicum, tomato and beans. Stir in the basil.
3 To make the dressing, shake the ingredients in a jar until combined. Pour over the salad and toss to coat.
4 Preheat the oven to moderate 180°C (350°F/Gas 4). Using a small knife, cut cactus shapes or large triangles out of the tortillas, brush lightly with the oil and sprinkle with Parmesan. Bake for 5–10 minutes, or until crisp and golden.
5 To make the guacamole, mash the avocados with the lemon juice. Add the garlic, onion, chilli, sour cream and taco sauce and mix well.
6 Put the salad in a large bowl or on a platter, pile the guacamole in the centre, top with the sour cream and arrange the cactus shapes on top.

NUTRITION PER SERVE (12)
Protein 15 g; Fat 25 g; Carbohydrate 40 g; Dietary Fibre 10 g; Cholesterol 15 mg; 1735 kJ (415 cal)

Combine the sweet potato with the onion, capsicum, tomato and beans.

Using a small sharp knife, cut cactus shapes out of the tortillas.

SMOKED COD AND LENTIL SALAD

Preparation time: 25 minutes
Total cooking time: 45 minutes
Serves 6

250 g (8 oz) brown lentils
1 onion, finely chopped
1 bay leaf
500 g (1 lb) smoked cod
1/4 cup (15 g/1/2 oz) chopped
  dill
3 spring onions, chopped
100 g (31/4 oz) sweet spiced
  gherkins, chopped
100 g (31/4 oz) sun-dried
  capsicum, chopped

Dressing
2 cloves garlic, crushed
2 tablespoons whole egg
  mayonnaise
1/4 cup (60 g/2 oz) plain yoghurt
2 tablespoons chopped chives

1 Place the lentils, onion and bay leaf in a pan, cover with water and bring to the boil. Reduce the heat and simmer for 25–30 minutes, or until the lentils are just tender. Drain and set aside to cool. Do not overcook the lentils or they will become mushy.

2 Half fill a frying pan with water. Bring to the boil and add the smoked cod. Reduce the heat and simmer gently for 10 minutes, or until it flakes when tested with a fork. Drain and allow to cool slightly before breaking into large pieces.

3 Add the dill, spring onion, gherkin and capsicum to the lentils, then gently fold in the cod pieces.

4 To make the dressing, combine the ingredients in a bowl and whisk until smooth. Pour over the salad and lightly toss to coat.

NUTRITION PER SERVE
Protein 25 g; Fat 4 g; Carbohydrate 25 g; Dietary Fibre 7 g; Cholesterol 45 mg; 1005 kJ (240 cal)

COOK'S FILE

Note: Smoked cod is available from most supermarkets or fish markets. Make this salad up to 3 hours ahead. Add the dressing just before serving.

Cover the lentils, onion and bay leaf with water, and bring to the boil.

Gently simmer the smoked cod for 10 minutes, or until it flakes with a fork.

Add the dill, spring onion, gherkin and capsicum to the lentils and onion.

TORTELLINI SALAD WITH BALSAMIC VINAIGRETTE

Preparation time: 15 minutes
+ 20 minutes standing
Total cooking time: 8 minutes
Serves 4

Balsamic Vinaigrette
1/4 cup (60 ml/2 fl oz) olive oil
2 tablespoons balsamic vinegar
1 clove garlic, crushed

375 g (12 oz) spinach and
ricotta tortellini
6 spring onions, thinly sliced
100 g (3 1/4 oz) pitted black and
green olives, finely diced
6 egg (Roma) tomatoes, finely
diced
2 tablespoons chopped parsley
8–12 black olives, to garnish

1 To make the vinaigrette, combine the oil, vinegar and garlic, and season to taste with salt and freshly ground black pepper.
2 Cook the tortellini in a large pan with plenty of salted boiling water until tender. Drain the tortellini and rinse under cold water. Drain again.
3 Combine the sliced spring onion, diced olives and tomato, and toss with the dressing in a large bowl.
4 Add the tortellini and set aside for at least 20 minutes to allow the flavours to develop. Toss the parsley through the salad and season with salt and freshly ground black pepper. Transfer to a serving bowl and serve garnished with the black olives.

NUTRITION PER SERVE
Protein 15 g; Fat 20 g; Carbohydrate 70 g;
Dietary Fibre 7 g; Cholesterol 2 mg;
2125 kJ (505 cal)

Slice the spring onions thinly, and finely dice the pitted olives.

Add the dressing to the combined spring onion, olives and tomato.

Add the cooked tortellini to the tossed salad and dressing.

COCONUT AND CHICKPEA SALAD

Preparation time: 15 minutes
Total cooking time: Nil
Serves 6–8

1 green mango, diced
1 green chilli, finely chopped
2 x 380 g (12¼ oz) cans chickpeas, rinsed and drained
¼ cup (25 g/¾ oz) desiccated coconut

¼ cup (15 g/½ oz) roughly chopped coriander

Dressing
1 clove garlic, crushed
¼ cup (60 ml/2 fl oz) coconut milk
3 teaspoons fish sauce
2 tablespoons lime juice
1 teaspoon grated fresh ginger
1 teaspoon sugar

1 Combine the mango with the chilli, chickpeas, coconut and coriander.

2 To make the dressing, shake the ingredients together in a screw-top jar to combine.
3 Pour the dressing over the salad, cover and refrigerate for up to 3 hours to allow the flavours to develop.

NUTRITION PER SERVE (8)
Protein 4 g; Fat 5 g; Carbohydrate 10 g;
Dietary Fibre 3 g; Cholesterol 0 mg;
400 kJ (95 cal)

COOK'S FILE

Note: If green mango is not available, use a firm, underripe mango.

Peel the mango and, using a sharp knife, dice the flesh.

Wearing a glove to protect your hand, chop the chilli finely.

Shake the dressing in a screw-top jar, then pour over the salad.

EGG AND BACON PASTA SALAD

Preparation time: 20 minutes
Total cooking time: 20 minutes
Serves 4–6

350 g (11¼ oz) fettucine
oil, for cooking
250 g (8 oz) bacon, cut into thin
strips
3 eggs, beaten
3 spring onions, finely chopped

Dressing
¼ cup (60 g/2 oz) sour cream
1 tablespoon cream
1 tablespoon white wine vinegar
2 tablespoons chopped parsley

1 Add the pasta and a little oil to a large pan of boiling salted water. Cook until al dente. Drain and allow to cool.
2 Fry the bacon in a hot heavy-based frying pan for 4 minutes, or until crisp. Drain on paper towels. Reheat the pan, add 1 tablespoon oil and pour in the eggs, swirling to cover the pan.

Cook for 2 minutes, or until set. Turn over and cook for 30 seconds. Remove from the pan and allow to cool. Cut into thin strips.
3 To make the dressing, whisk the sour cream, cream, vinegar, parsley and salt and pepper to taste. Put the pasta, bacon, egg and dressing in a large bowl and toss to combine. Scatter with the spring onion.

NUTRITION PER SERVE (6)
Protein 20 g; Fat 15 g; Carbohydrate 40 g; Dietary Fibre 3 g; Cholesterol 130 mg; 1660 kJ (395 cal)

Using a sharp knife, cut the bacon into thin strips.

Add the pasta to a large pan of boiling salted water and cook until al dente.

Cook the eggs until set, then turn over and cook the other side.

CARAMELISED ONION AND POTATO SALAD

Preparation time: 20 minutes
Total cooking time: 50 minutes
Serves 10–12

oil, for cooking
6 red onions, thinly sliced
1 kg (2 lb) kipfler potatoes
4 rashers bacon
30 g (1 oz) chives, snipped

Mayonnaise
1 cup (250 g/8 oz) whole egg
    mayonnaise

1 tablespoon Dijon mustard
juice of 1 lemon
2 tablespoons sour cream

1 Heat 2 tablespoons of oil in a large heavy-based frying pan, add the sliced onion and cook over medium heat for 40 minutes, or until caramelised.
2 Cut the potatoes into large chunks (if they are small leave them whole). Cook in boiling water until just tender, then drain and allow to cool slightly. Do not overcook the potatoes or they will fall apart.
3 Grill the bacon until crisp, drain on paper towels and allow to cool slightly before coarsely chopping.

4 Put the potato, onion and chives in a large bowl, reserving a few chives for garnishing, and toss to combine.
5 To make the mayonnaise, put the ingredients in a bowl and whisk to combine. Pour over the salad and toss to coat. Sprinkle with the bacon and garnish with the reserved chives.

NUTRITION PER SERVE (12)
Protein 6 g; Fat 10 g; Carbohydrate 20 g; Dietary Fibre 3 g; Cholesterol 15 mg; 835 kJ (200 cal)

COOK'S FILE

Note: Kipflers are small, elongated potatoes. Other waxy potatoes, such as pontiac or Desiree, may be used.

Heat the oil and cook the sliced red onion until it is caramelised.

Cut the potatoes into large chunks before cooking in boiling water.

Whisk the mayonnaise, mustard, lemon juice and sour cream until combined.

BLACK BEAN AND AVOCADO SALAD

Preparation time: 20 minutes
  + overnight soaking
Total cooking time: 55 minutes
Serves 6

1 cup (220 g/7 oz) black beans
1 fresh corn cob
1 tomato, chopped
1/2 cup (15 g/1/2 oz) coriander
  leaves
1 red onion, sliced
1 red capsicum, thinly sliced
2 avocados, thinly sliced

Lime Dressing
100 ml (3 1/4 fl oz) lime juice
1/4 cup (60 ml/2 fl oz) olive oil
1 tablespoon chopped coriander

1 Place the beans in a large bowl and cover with cold water. Leave to soak overnight. Drain and place in a large pan of water. Bring to the boil, then simmer for 45 minutes, or until the beans are tender. Drain and cool.
2 Cook the corn in a large pan of boiling water for 8–10 minutes, or until tender. Drain and cool. Cut off the kernels with a sharp knife.
3 Place the beans, tomato, coriander, corn, red onion and capsicum in a large bowl. Toss until well combined.
4 To make the dressing, put the lime juice, olive oil and chopped coriander in a screw-top jar and shake until combined. Pour into the bean salad and toss gently to combine. Arrange the avocado slices on individual plates or a large serving platter and top with the black bean salad.

NUTRITION PER SERVE
Protein 7 g; Fat 30 g; Carbohydrate 9 g; Dietary Fibre 5 g; Cholesterol 0 mg; 1395 kJ (330 cal)

COOK'S FILE

Note: Black beans are available from supermarkets and health food stores.

Cover the black beans with cold water in a large bowl.

Cut the cooked corn kernels off the cob with a large sharp knife.

Combine the beans, tomato, coriander, corn, red onion and capsicum.

MEDITERRANEAN PASTA SALAD WITH BLACK OLIVE DRESSING

Preparation time: 30 minutes
Total cooking time: 25 minutes
Serves 4

250 g (8 oz) fusilli pasta
1 red capsicum
1 yellow or green capsicum
1 tablespoon sunflower oil
2 tablespoons olive oil
2 cloves garlic, crushed
1 eggplant, cubed
2 zucchini, thickly sliced
2 large ripe tomatoes, peeled,
   seeded and chopped
1/4 cup (7 g/1/4 oz) chopped flat-
   leaf parsley
1 teaspoon seasoned pepper
150 g (5 oz) feta cheese,
   crumbled

Black Olive Dressing
6 large marinated black olives,
   pitted
1/2 cup (125 ml/4 fl oz) olive oil
2 tablespoons balsamic vinegar

1 Add the fusilli pasta to a large pan of gently boiling water and cook for 10–12 minutes, or until al dente. Drain, spread in a single layer on a baking tray to dry, then refrigerate, uncovered, until chilled.
2 Cut the red and yellow capsicum in half lengthways, removing the seeds and white membrane, then cut into large pieces. Place, skin-side-up, under a hot grill until the skin blackens and blisters. Leave under a tea towel or in a plastic bag to cool, then peel away and discard the skin. Slice the flesh into thick strips.

3 Heat the sunflower and olive oil in a frying pan. Add the garlic and eggplant and fry quickly, tossing constantly, until lightly browned. Remove from the heat and place in a large bowl. Steam or microwave the zucchini for 1–2 minutes, or until just tender. Rinse under cold water, drain, and add to the eggplant.
4 To make the dressing, process the olives in a food processor until finely chopped. Gradually add the olive oil, processing until thoroughly combined

after each addition. Add the vinegar, season with salt and freshly ground black pepper and process to combine.
5 Combine the pasta, capsicum, eggplant, zucchini, tomato, parsley and pepper in a large bowl. Spoon onto individual serving plates or a large salad platter, top with the feta cheese and drizzle with the dressing.

NUTRITION PER SERVE
Protein 15 g; Fat 55 g; Carbohydrate 50 g;
Dietary Fibre 8 g; Cholesterol 25 mg;
3220 kJ (765 cal)

Drain the cooked pasta and spread on a tray to dry.

Remove the seeds and white membrane from the halved capsicums.

Fry the cubed eggplant quickly until it is lightly browned.

SPICY BASMATI RICE, CASHEW AND GREEN PEA SALAD

Preparation time: 30 minutes
 + 30 minutes standing
Total cooking time: 20 minutes
Serves 6

40 g (1¼ oz) butter or ghee
½ teaspoon turmeric
300 g (10 oz) basmati rice
½ teaspoon salt
200 g (6½ oz) fresh or frozen
 peas, thawed
¼ cup (60 ml/2 fl oz) peanut oil
1 teaspoon yellow mustard
 seeds
1 teaspoon cumin seeds
¼ cup (35 g/1¼ oz) currants
1 clove garlic, crushed
1–2 small green chillies, finely
 chopped
1 teaspoon Madras curry
 powder
100 ml (3¼ fl oz) coconut
 cream
50 g (1¾ oz) glacé ginger, cut
 into thin strips
¼ small red onion, finely
 chopped
1 tablespoon chopped mint
 leaves
1 tablespoon chopped coriander
½ cup (30 g/1 oz) shredded
 coconut
100 g (3¼ oz) roasted cashew
 nuts, coarsely chopped
2 teaspoons shredded coconut,
 to garnish

1 Melt the butter or ghee in a heavy-based pan and stir in the turmeric. Add the rice and salt, and stir for 10–15 seconds, then pour in 1½ cups (375 ml/12 fl oz) of water. Stir over high heat until boiling, then reduce the heat until gently simmering. Simmer, tightly covered, and cook for 13 minutes without removing the lid. Remove the pan from the heat and leave for 10 minutes without removing the lid, then fluff gently with a fork. Add the peas, transfer to a large bowl and allow to cool.
2 Heat 2 teaspoons of the oil in a pan and stir in the mustard and cumin seeds. When the mustard seeds start to pop, add the currants, garlic, chilli and curry powder. Stir to combine, but do not brown. Stir in the coconut cream, remove from the heat and transfer to the bowl of rice and peas.

3 Add the ginger, onion, herbs and the remaining oil. Toss well, and set aside for at least 30 minutes. Just before serving, toss through the coconut and cashew nuts. Garnish with the shredded coconut.

NUTRITION PER SERVE
Protein 9 g; Fat 30 g; Carbohydrate 55 g; Dietary Fibre 6 g; Cholesterol 15 mg; 2110 kJ (500 cal)

COOK'S FILE

Note: Rice salads often improve if made in advance, and this one is no exception. It may be prepared up to 24 hours in advance, but add the cashew nuts and coconut just before serving to ensure a crisp texture.

Cut the glacé ginger into thin strips, and chop the red onion and mint.

Add the rice and salt to the melted butter and turmeric.

Add the currants, garlic, chilli and curry powder to the mustard and cumin seeds.

Mayonnaises

BASIC MAYONNAISE

Place 2 egg yolks, 2 teaspoons Dijon mustard and 2 teaspoons lemon juice in a food processor or blender and process for 30 seconds, or until light and creamy. Add 1 cup (250 ml/8 fl oz) olive oil in a thin, steady stream, increasing the flow as the mayonnaise thickens. Stir in 2–4 teaspoons lemon juice and season with salt and freshly ground white pepper. Makes about 1¼ cups (310 g/10 oz)

NUTRITION PER 100 g: Protein 2 g; Fat 80 g; Carbohydrate 0 g; Dietary Fibre 0 g; Cholesterol 115 mg; 3040 kJ (725 cal)

GARLIC MAYONNAISE

Place 2 egg yolks, 2 teaspoons lemon juice and 2 crushed cloves garlic in a food processor or blender and process for 30 seconds, or until light and creamy. Gradually add 1 cup (250 ml/8 fl oz) olive oil in a thin stream. Increase the amount of oil added as the mayonnaise thickens. Stir in 2 teaspoons lemon juice and season with salt and freshly ground black pepper. Makes about 1¼ cups (310 g/10 oz)

NUTRITION PER 100 g: Protein 2 g; Fat 85 g; Carbohydrate 0 g; Dietary Fibre 0 g; Cholesterol 120 mg; 3110 kJ (740 cal)

MUSTARD MAYONNAISE

Place 2 egg yolks, 2 teaspoons white wine vinegar, 2 teaspoons Dijon mustard and 2 tablespoons wholegrain mustard in a food processor or blender and process for 30 seconds, or until light and creamy. Gradually add 1 cup (250 ml/8 fl oz) olive oil in a thin stream. Increase the amount of oil added as the mayonnaise thickens. Stir in 2 teaspoons white wine vinegar, 1/2 teaspoon honey and 1 tablespoon chopped tarragon (optional). Season with salt and freshly ground white pepper. Makes about 1¹/₃ cups (340 g/10³/4 oz)

NUTRITION PER 100 g: Protein 2 g; Fat 70 g; Carbohydrate 2 g; Dietary Fibre 1 g; Cholesterol 100 mg; 2705 kJ (645 cal)

Top row: Basic Mayonnaise; Mustard Mayonnaise (large picture); Spicy Mayonnaise; Green Goddess Dressing
Bottom row: Garlic Mayonnaise; Lime and Yoghurt Mayonnaise; Roasted Red Capsicum Mayonnaise

SPICY MAYONNAISE

Process 2 egg yolks and 2 teaspoons lime juice in a food processor or blender for 30 seconds, or until light and creamy. Gradually add 1 cup (250 ml/8 fl oz) olive oil in a thin stream. Increase the amount of oil added as the mayonnaise thickens. Stir in 1/4 teaspoon chilli flakes, 1/4 cup (15 g/1/2 oz) chopped coriander, 1 teaspoon grated fresh ginger and 1 tablespoon lime juice. Season with salt. Makes about 1 1/4 cups (310 g/10 oz)

NUTRITION PER 100 g: Protein 2 g; Fat 75 g; Carbohydrate 0 g; Dietary Fibre 0 g; Cholesterol 110 mg; 2895 kJ (690 cal)

LIME AND YOGHURT MAYONNAISE

Combine 1/2 cup (125 g/4 oz) each of ready-made whole egg mayonnaise and plain yoghurt. Mix in the rind and juice of 1 lime. Makes 1 cup (250 g/8 oz)

NUTRITION PER 100 g: Protein 2 g; Fat 15 g; Carbohydrate 9 g; Dietary Fibre 1 g; Cholesterol 15 mg; 690 kJ (165 cal)

GREEN GODDESS DRESSING

To 1 quantity of the basic mayonnaise add 4 finely chopped anchovy fillets, 1 crushed clove garlic, 1/4 cup (60 g/2 oz) sour cream and 1/4 cup (15 g/1/2 oz) chopped fresh herbs. Makes about 1 3/4 cups (435 g/13 3/4 oz)

NUTRITION PER 100 g: Protein 3 g; Fat 60 g; Carbohydrate 2 g; Dietary Fibre 2 g; Cholesterol 100 mg; 2325 kJ (555 cal)

ROASTED RED CAPSICUM MAYONNAISE

Cut 2 red capsicums into large pieces, removing the seeds and membrane. Place, skin-side-up, under a hot grill until the skin blackens and blisters. Cool in a plastic bag, then peel away the skin. Chop the flesh very finely and combine with 1/2 cup (125 g/4 oz) ready-made whole egg mayonnaise and 1 crushed clove garlic. Season with salt and black pepper. Makes about 2/3 cup (160 g/5 1/4 oz)

NUTRITION PER 100 g: Protein 1 g; Fat 10 g; Carbohydrate 9 g; Dietary Fibre 1 g; Cholesterol 10 mg; 550 kJ (130 cal)

RED LENTIL TABOULI

Preparation time: 25 minutes
+ 30 minutes standing
Total cooking time: 5 minutes
Serves 4–6

3/4 cup (130 g/4 1/4 oz) burghul
1 cup (250 g/8 oz) red lentils
1/2 cup (30 g/1 oz) finely
chopped flat-leaf parsley
1 cup (50 g/1 3/4 oz) finely
chopped coriander
1 red onion, finely chopped
2 large, firm, ripe tomatoes,
peeled, seeded and finely
chopped
1 stem lemon grass, white part
only, finely sliced
1/3 cup (80 ml/2 3/4 fl oz) light
olive oil
1/3 cup (80 ml/2 3/4 fl oz) lime
juice
1/4 teaspoon ground paprika

1 Place the burghul in a large bowl, cover with cold water and leave for 30 minutes. Drain through a fine sieve, pressing down with the back of a spoon to extract any moisture. Spread out on a cloth or paper towels and leave to dry while preparing the remaining salad.
2 Mix the lentils with 3 cups (750 ml/ 24 fl oz) water in a medium pan and bring to the boil. Reduce the heat and simmer for 5 minutes, or until tender. Drain and cool.
3 Combine the soaked burghul with the lentils, parsley, coriander, onion, tomato and lemon grass in a large bowl, and mix well. Whisk the oil, lime juice and paprika together in a small jug, season with salt and freshly ground black pepper and pour over

the salad. Fork through the salad and refrigerate before serving. Serve with crisp salad leaves.

NUTRITION PER SERVE (6)
Protein 15 g; Fat 15 g; Carbohydrate 30 g; Dietary Fibre 10 g; Cholesterol 0 mg; 1260 kJ (300 cal)

COOK'S FILE

Note: To prepare the lentils in the microwave, add to 3 cups (750 ml/ 24 fl oz) water in a microwave-safe bowl and cook on high (100%) for 5 minutes, stirring occasionally. Remove, drain and cool.

Finely slice the stem of lemon grass, using only the white part.

Press the soaked burghul against a fine sieve to remove any excess moisture.

Combine the burghul, lentils, herbs, onion, tomato and lemon grass.

SUCCULENT CHICKEN AND PASTA SALAD

Preparation time: 30 minutes
Total cooking time: 25 minutes
Serves 4

250 g (8 oz) chicken breast fillet
1¹/₂ cups (375 ml/12 fl oz)
    chicken stock
350 g (11¹/₄ oz) fusilli pasta
155 g (5 oz) fresh asparagus,
    cut into short lengths
150 g (5 oz) Gruyère cheese,
    grated
2 spring onions, finely sliced

Dressing
¹/₄ cup (60 ml/2 fl oz) olive oil
¹/₄ cup (60 ml/2 fl oz) lemon
    juice
¹/₂ teaspoon sugar

1 Put the chicken and stock in a frying pan. Bring to the boil, reduce the heat and poach gently, turning regularly, for 8 minutes, or until tender. Remove, cool and slice thinly.
2 Cook the pasta in a large pan of boiling salted water for 10–12 minutes, or until al dente. Drain and cool.
3 Cook the asparagus in boiling water for 2 minutes. Drain and place in a bowl of iced water. Drain again. Combine with the chicken, pasta and cheese in a large bowl.
4 To make the dressing, whisk the ingredients together. Season with salt and pepper. Add to the salad and toss well. Transfer to a serving bowl and scatter with the spring onions.

NUTRITION PER SERVE
Protein 40 g; Fat 30 g; Carbohydrate 60 g;
Dietary Fibre 5 g; Cholesterol 70 mg;
2785 kJ (665 cal)

Grate the cheese, chop the asparagus and finely slice the spring onion.

Pour the stock over the chicken and poach over low heat, turning regularly.

Cook the asparagus in a small pan of boiling water.

BEAN SALAD WITH CUMIN AND CORIANDER DRESSING

Preparation time: 25 minutes
Total cooking time: 15 minutes
Serves 6

300 g (10 oz) vegetable spiral
  pasta
2 tablespoons sunflower oil
1 leek, sliced
1 red capsicum, seeded and
  diced
2 cups (130 g/4¼ oz) finely
  shredded English spinach
150 g (5 oz) button mushrooms,
  halved
300 g (10 oz) can red kidney
  beans, rinsed and drained
300 g (10 oz) can butter beans,
  rinsed and drained
2 tablespoons snipped chives
½ teaspoon coarsely ground
  black pepper
60 g (2 oz) sunflower seeds,
  toasted

Cumin and Coriander Dressing
2 cloves garlic, crushed
½ teaspoon ground cumin
½ teaspoon ground coriander
2 tablespoons cider vinegar
½ cup (125 ml/4 fl oz) olive oil

1 Cook the pasta in a large pan of boiling water for 8–10 minutes, or until al dente. Drain.
2 Heat the oil in a large pan, add the leek and capsicum and stir-fry over medium heat for 2–3 minutes. Add the spinach and mushrooms and toss together for about 1 minute, or until the spinach just wilts.
3 To make the dressing, mix the garlic, cumin, coriander and vinegar together. Gradually add the olive oil and whisk to combine.
4 In a large bowl, combine the pasta, vegetables, beans, chives and black pepper. Pour in the dressing and toss through. Transfer to a serving bowl and sprinkle with the sunflower seeds.

NUTRITION PER SERVE
Protein 15 g; Fat 30 g; Carbohydrate 45 g; Dietary Fibre 10 g; Cholesterol 0 mg; 2215 kJ (525 cal)

Add the spinach and mushrooms to the leek and capsicum.

Gradually whisk the oil into the combined garlic, cumin, coriander and vinegar.

Pour the dressing into the salad and toss gently to mix through.

AVOCADO, SALMON AND COUSCOUS SALAD

Preparation time: 15 minutes
Total cooking time: Nil
Serves 4

Dressing
1/3 cup (80 ml/2³/4 fl oz) olive oil
2 tablespoons lemon juice

1 cup (185 g/6 oz) couscous
2 teaspoons olive oil
³/4 cup (185 ml/6 fl oz) boiling
   chicken stock

2 tablespoons finely chopped
   preserved lemon
2 tablespoons chopped chives
2 avocados
100 g (3¹/4 oz) sliced smoked
   salmon

1 To make the dressing, put the olive oil and lemon juice in a small bowl and whisk to combine. Season to taste with salt and pepper.
2 Place the couscous and oil in a bowl and add the boiling stock. Stir, cover and leave for 10 minutes. Add the preserved lemon, chopped chives, freshly ground black pepper to taste,

and 2 tablespoons of the dressing. Stir through using a fork to separate the couscous grains. Leave to cool.
3 Spoon the couscous onto individual serving plates. Halve the avocados and remove the seeds. Carefully peel away the skin and cut the avocados into quarters. Arrange over the couscous and lay the slices of salmon over the avocado. Drizzle with the dressing and serve immediately. Delicious with lemon wedges.

NUTRITION PER SERVE
Protein 10 g; Fat 50 g; Carbohydrate 25 g; Dietary Fibre 2 g; Cholesterol 10 mg; 2460 kJ (585 cal)

Using a sharp knife, finely chop the preserved lemon.

Add the boiling stock to the combined couscous and oil.

Halve the avocados and remove the seeds with a sharp-bladed knife.

POTATO AND SMOKED SALMON SALAD

Preparation time: 15 minutes
Total cooking time: 15 minutes
Serves 6

750 g (1¹/₂ 1b) baby new
   potatoes
100 g (3¹/₄ oz) sliced smoked
   salmon, cut into strips
2 Lebanese cucumbers, sliced
2 tablespoons caper berries or
   pickled capers
5 spring onions, sliced
2 tablespoons salmon roe, to
   garnish

Dressing
¹/₃ cup (80 ml/2³/₄ fl oz) olive oil
1 tablespoon lemon juice
¹/₂ teaspoon caster sugar

1 Add the potatoes to a large pan of boiling water and cook until just tender. Drain and leave to cool but do not refrigerate. If the potatoes are large, cut them in half.
2 To make the dressing, place the olive oil, lemon juice and sugar in a small bowl and whisk to combine.
3 Place the potatoes in a large bowl with the smoked salmon, cucumber, caper berries and spring onion. Add the dressing and toss gently to combine. Garnish with the salmon roe and serve immediately.

NUTRITION PER SERVE
Protein 8 g; Fat 15 g; Carbohydrate 20 g; Dietary Fibre 3 g; Cholesterol 30 mg; 985 kJ (235 cal)

COOK'S FILE

Note: Small waxy potatoes, such as pink eyes, are suitable for this recipe.

Using a sharp knife, cut the smoked salmon slices into thin strips.

Insert the tip of a knife to test if the potatoes are tender.

Add the spring onion to the potatoes, salmon, cucumber and caper berries.

GRILLED EGGPLANT AND CHICKPEA SALAD

Preparation time: 20 minutes
Total cooking time: 10 minutes
Serves 4

Dressing
2 tablespoons tahini
2 tablespoons lemon juice
1 clove garlic, crushed
1/2 teaspoon ground cumin
1/3 cup (80 ml/2³/4 fl oz) olive oil

2 x 300 g (10 oz) cans chickpeas, drained
1 red capsicum, cut into thin strips
3 spring onions, sliced
2 tablespoons chopped flat-leaf parsley
6 slender eggplants, diagonally sliced
olive oil, for brushing
4 thin slices prosciutto

1 To make the dressing, combine the tahini, lemon juice, garlic and cumin. Gradually add the oil and whisk until combined. Season with salt and pepper.
2 Preheat the grill. Put the chickpeas, capsicum, spring onion and parsley in a bowl. Add the dressing, toss gently and transfer to a shallow serving dish.
3 Brush the eggplant lightly with the oil and grill until tender and browned. Grill the prosciutto slices until crisp.
4 Arrange the eggplant over the chickpea mixture, crumble the prosciutto over the top and serve.

NUTRITION PER SERVE
Protein 10 g; Fat 25 g; Carbohydrate 15 g; Dietary Fibre 8 g; Cholesterol 9 mg; 1415 kJ (335 cal)

Combine the tahini, lemon juice, garlic and cumin, and gradually add the oil.

Slice the eggplants diagonally and brush lightly with the olive oil.

Grill the prosciutto on a baking tray until it is crisp.

THAI NOODLE SALAD

Preparation time: 25 minutes
Total cooking time: 5 minutes
Serves 4

Dressing
2 tablespoons grated fresh
    ginger
2 tablespoons soy sauce
2 tablespoons sesame oil
1/3 cup (80 ml/2³/4 fl oz) red
    wine vinegar
3–4 teaspoons sweet chilli sauce
2 cloves garlic, crushed
1/3 cup (80 ml/2³/4 fl oz) kecap
    manis (see Note)

250 g (8 oz) fine instant noodles
5 spring onions, sliced
2 tablespoons chopped coriander
1 red capsicum, chopped
100 g (3¹/4 oz) snow peas, sliced
500 g (1 lb) cooked king
    prawns, peeled, halved and
    deveined

1 To make the dressing, put the ingredients in a large bowl and whisk with a fork to combine.
2 Cook the noodles in a large pan of boiling water for 2 minutes and drain well. Add to the dressing and toss to combine. Leave to cool.
3 Add the remaining ingredients to the noodles and toss gently. Serve at room temperature.

NUTRITION PER SERVE
Protein 35 g; Fat 15 g; Carbohydrate 60 g; Dietary Fibre 3 g; Cholesterol 235 mg; 2275 kJ (540 cal)

C O O K ' S   F I L E

Note: Kecap manis (sweet soy sauce) is available from Asian food stores.

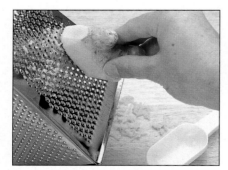

Peel and finely grate the fresh ginger on the fine side of the grater.

Add the kecap manis to the other ingredients and mix to combine.

Add the noodles to a large pan of boiling water and cook until tender.

SPICY INDIAN-STYLE LENTIL SALAD

Preparation time: 30 minutes
Total cooking time: 1 hour 10 minutes
Serves 6

1 cup (220 g/7 oz) brown rice
1 cup (185 g/6 oz) brown lentils
1 teaspoon turmeric
1 teaspoon ground cinnamon
6 cardamom pods
3 star anise
2 bay leaves
1/4 cup (60 ml/2 fl oz) sunflower oil
1 tablespoon lemon juice
250 g (8 oz) broccoli florets
2 carrots, cut into julienne strips
1 onion, finely chopped
2 cloves garlic, crushed
1 red capsicum, finely chopped
1 teaspoon garam masala
1 teaspoon ground coriander
1 1/2 cups (235 g/7 1/4 oz) fresh or frozen peas, thawed

Mint and Yoghurt Dressing
1 cup (250 g/8 oz) plain yoghurt
1 tablespoon lemon juice
1 tablespoon finely chopped fresh mint
1 teaspoon cumin seeds

1 Put 3 cups (750 ml/24 fl oz) water with the rice, lentils, turmeric, cinnamon, cardamom, star anise and bay leaves in a medium pan. Stir to combine and bring to the boil. Reduce the heat, cover and simmer gently for 50–60 minutes, or until the liquid is absorbed. Remove the whole spices and discard. Transfer the mixture to a large bowl. Whisk 2 tablespoons of the oil with the lemon juice and fork through the rice mixture.
2 Boil, steam or microwave the broccoli and carrots until tender. Drain and refresh in cold water.
3 Heat the remaining oil in a large pan and add the onion, garlic and capsicum. Stir-fry for 2–3 minutes, then add the garam masala and coriander, and stir-fry for a further 1–2 minutes. Add the vegetables and toss to coat in the spice mixture. Add to the rice mixture and fork through to combine. Cover and refrigerate.
4 To make the dressing, mix the yoghurt, lemon juice, mint and cumin seeds together, and season with salt and pepper. Spoon the salad into individual serving bowls or onto a platter and serve with the dressing.

NUTRITION PER SERVE
Protein 20 g; Fat 15 g; Carbohydrate 50 g; Dietary Fibre 10 g; Cholesterol 7 mg; 1605 kJ (380 cal)

Add the cardamom pods, star anise and bay leaves to the pan.

Add the vegetables and toss to coat with the spice mixture.

Mix the yoghurt, lemon juice, mint and cumin seeds together.

109

TOMATO PASTA SALAD WITH THAI-STYLE VEGETABLES

Preparation time: 20 minutes
Total cooking time: 20 minutes
Serves 4–6

350 g (11¼ oz) tomato and herb fettucine or plain fettucine
100 g (3¼ oz) fresh baby corn, halved lengthways
1 carrot, cut into julienne strips (see Note)
200 g (6½ oz) broccoli, cut into small florets
½ red capsicum, cut into julienne strips
2 teaspoons sesame seeds
3 spring onions, chopped

Dressing
¼ cup (60 ml/2 fl oz) sweet chilli sauce
2 teaspoons fish sauce
¼ cup (90 g/3 oz) honey

1 Cook the pasta in a large pan of boiling salted water for 10–12 minutes, or until al dente. Drain and cool.
2 Cook the corn in boiling water for 1 minute. Remove and plunge into a bowl of iced water. Cook the carrot, broccoli and capsicum in boiling water for 30 seconds, then drain and add to the iced water to cool. Drain the vegetables and add to the pasta.
3 To make the dressing, whisk the ingredients together, drizzle over the salad and toss well. Sprinkle with the sesame seeds and spring onions.

NUTRITION PER SERVE (6)
Protein 10 g; Fat 1 g; Carbohydrate 60 g;
Dietary Fibre 6 g; Cholesterol 0 mg;
1260 kJ (300 cal)

COOK'S FILE

Note: Julienne strips are even-sized strips of vegetables, the size and shape of matchsticks.

Cut the broccoli into small florets and the other vegetables into strips.

Cook the carrot, broccoli and capsicum in boiling water for 30 seconds.

Whisk together the sweet chilli sauce, fish sauce and honey.

INDEX

INTERNATIONAL GLOSSARY OF INGREDIENTS

English spinach	spinach	daikon radish	mooli
burghul	cracked wheat	kecap manis	Indonesian sweet soy sauce
prawns	shrimp	mirin	sweet rice wine
tomato paste (Aus.)	tomato purée, double concentrate (UK)	tomato purée (Aus.)	sieved crushed tomatoes/ passata (UK)

Published by Murdoch Books®, a division of Murdoch Magazines Pty Limited,
213 Miller Street, North Sydney NSW 2060.

Managing Editor: Jane Price **Designer:** Annette Fitzgerald **Food Editor:** Dimitra Stais **Editors:** Alison Moss, Justine Upex
Recipe Development: Joanne Glynn, Michelle Lawton, Barbara Lowery, Rosemary Mellish, Dimitra Stais, Jody Vassallo
Home Economists: Anna Beaumont, Alex Diblasi, Michelle Lawton, Kerrie Mullins, Kerrie Ray **Photographers:** Tony Lyon,
Damien Wood, Reg Morrison (steps) **Food Stylist:** Marie-Hélène Clauzon **Food Preparation:** Kerrie Mullins
CEO & Publisher: Anne Wilson **International Sales Director:** Mark Newman

The nutritional information provided for each recipe does not include any accompaniments, such as rice, unless they are listed
in the ingredients. The values are approximations and can be affected by biological and seasonal variations in food, the
unknown composition of some manufactured foods and uncertainty in the dietary database. Nutrient data given are derived
primarily from the NUTTAB95 database produced by the Australian New Zealand Food Authority.

National Library of Australia Cataloguing-in-Publication Data. Family Circle step-by-step salads. Includes index.
ISBN 0 86411 656 X. 1. Salads. I. Family Circle (Sydney, N.S.W.). 641.83. First published 1997.
Printed by Prestige Litho, Queensland.